Creative Geometric Flowers and Patterns

A Coloring Book For The Novice To Help Learn Color Combinations

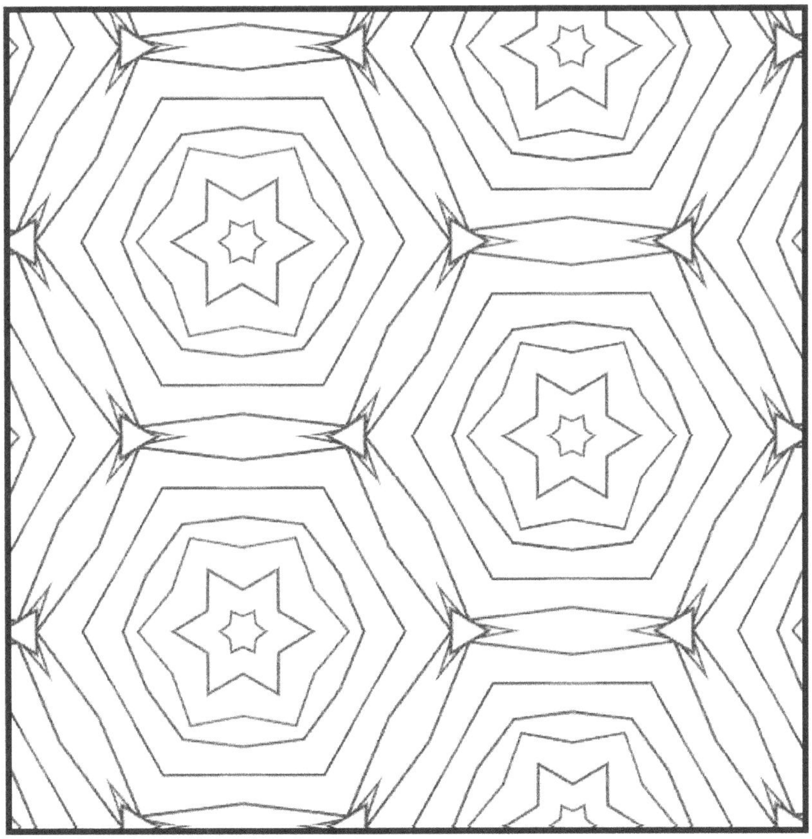

By: Kaye Dennan

KD Coloring Studio

ISBN-13: 978-1523673421

Publishers Notes

Disclaimer

A note from the Illustrator

Creative Geometric Patterns For The Novice

This book was developed especially for those who want to learn how to choose colors and who want to experiment with color flow.

The wide range of images in this book will give you the chance to extend your capacity for working with color and shapes.

These images will give you the opportunity to try out different color hues, shading, color combinations and will keep you occupied for hours.

Did you know that colors affect your emotions?

Most of us have favorite colors and they are favorites because we like how they make us feel when we see them or even wear them.

Basic relationships in the way colors affect us are listed below but the reality is that what might make one person feel cheerful can make another person feel irritated depending on the viewers' past experiences or cultural differences.

Warm Colors – Red, Orange, Yellow

Cool Colors – Green, Blue, Purple

Neutral Colors – Black, Gray, White, Tan, Brown

I encourage you to experiment with color and shapes and enjoy your coloring pass-time,

****

Every Second Page has been left blank so that you do not ruin one of your colored designs with color bleeding through the paper.

If you are using pencils then I would suggest you slide a piece of thin cardboard or thick paper under the page you are coloring just to prevent any pressure marks on the following page.

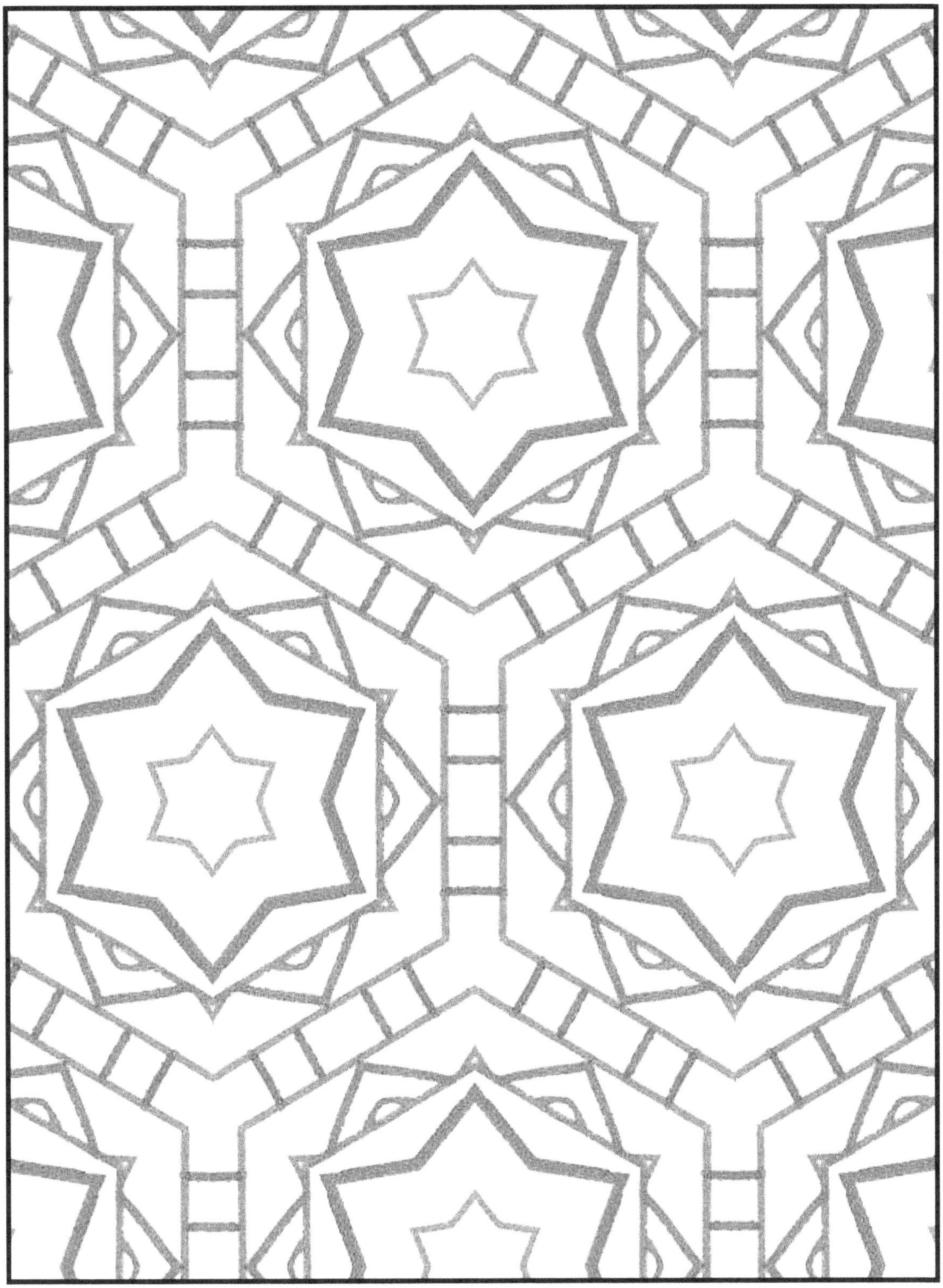

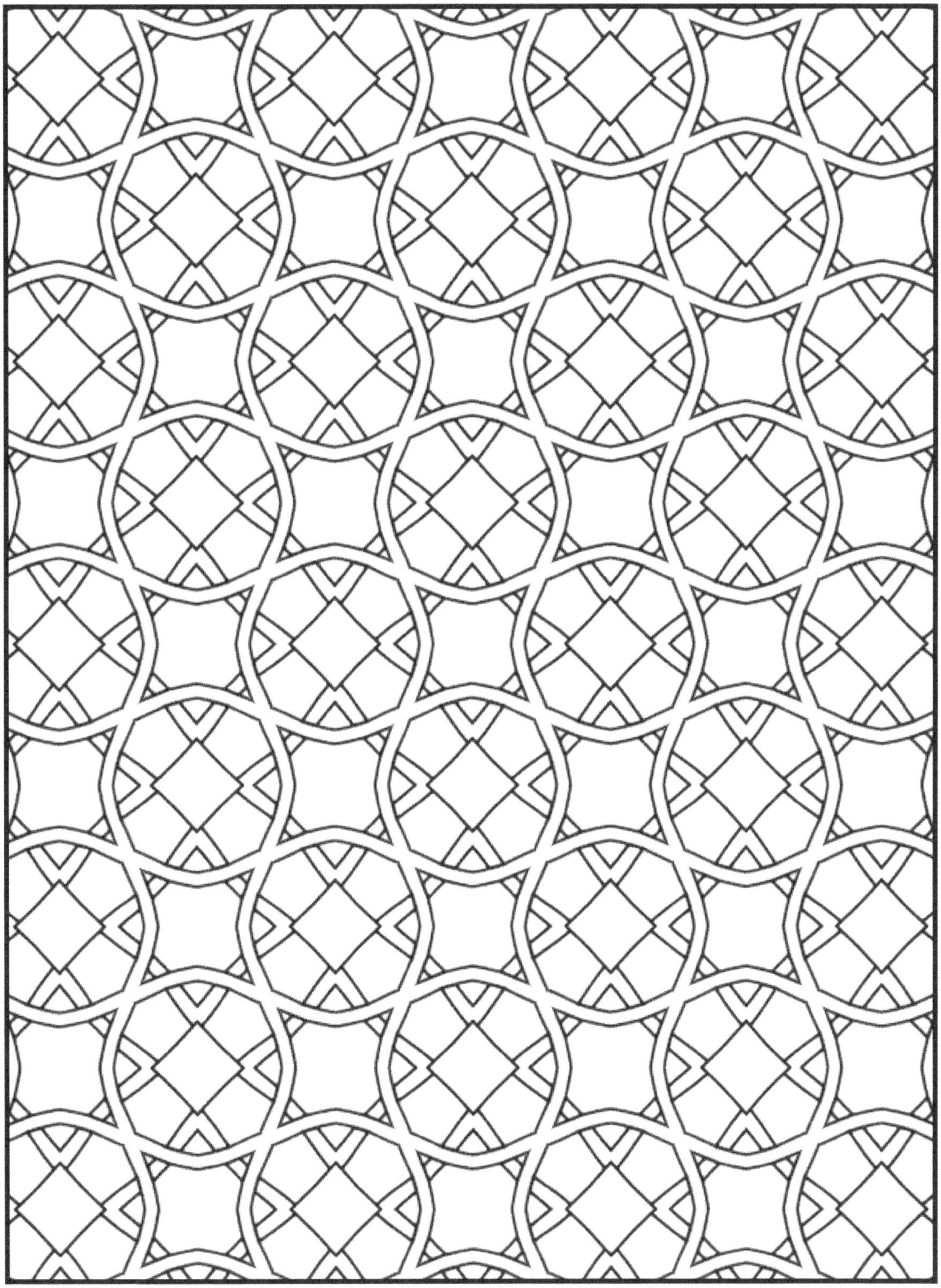

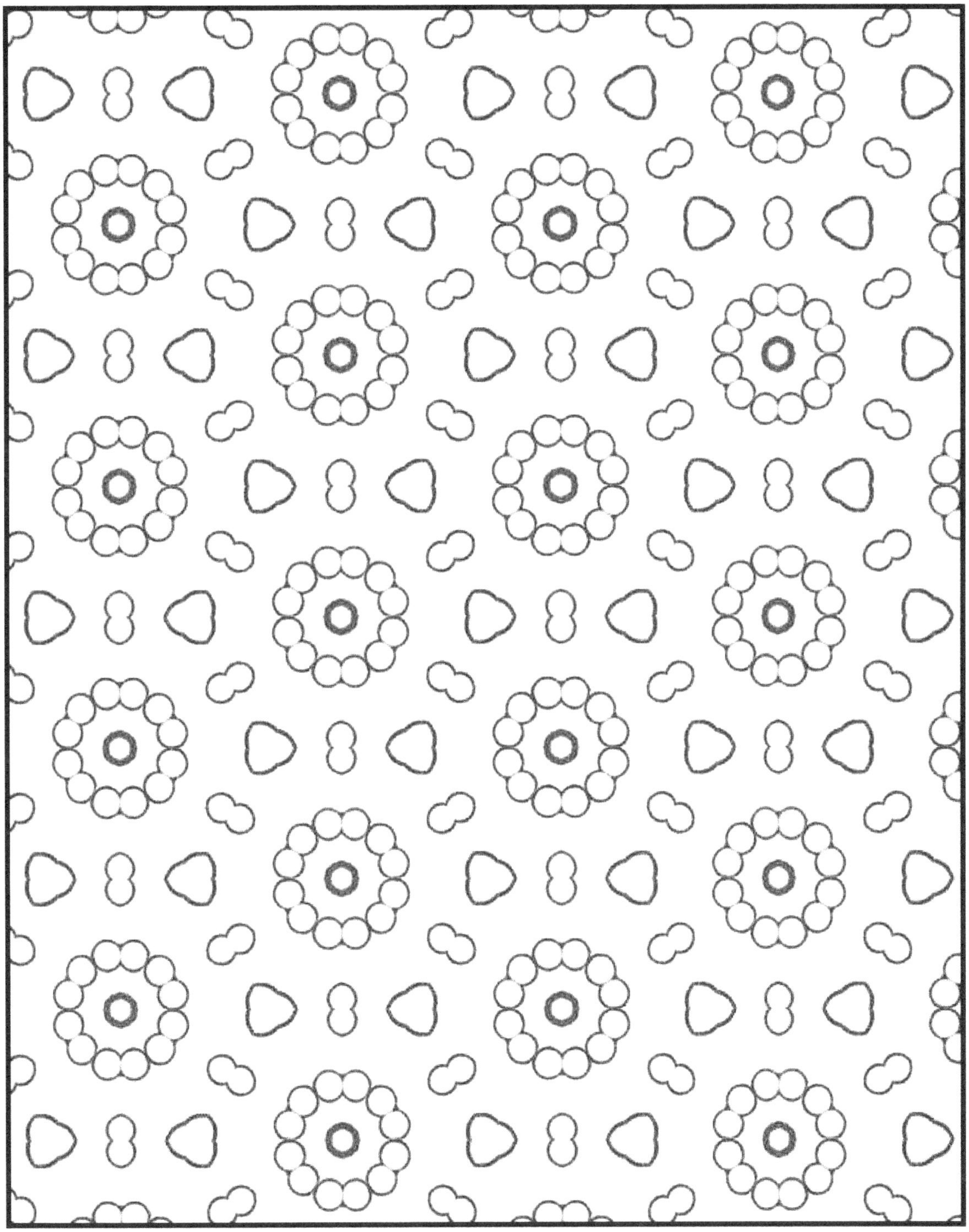

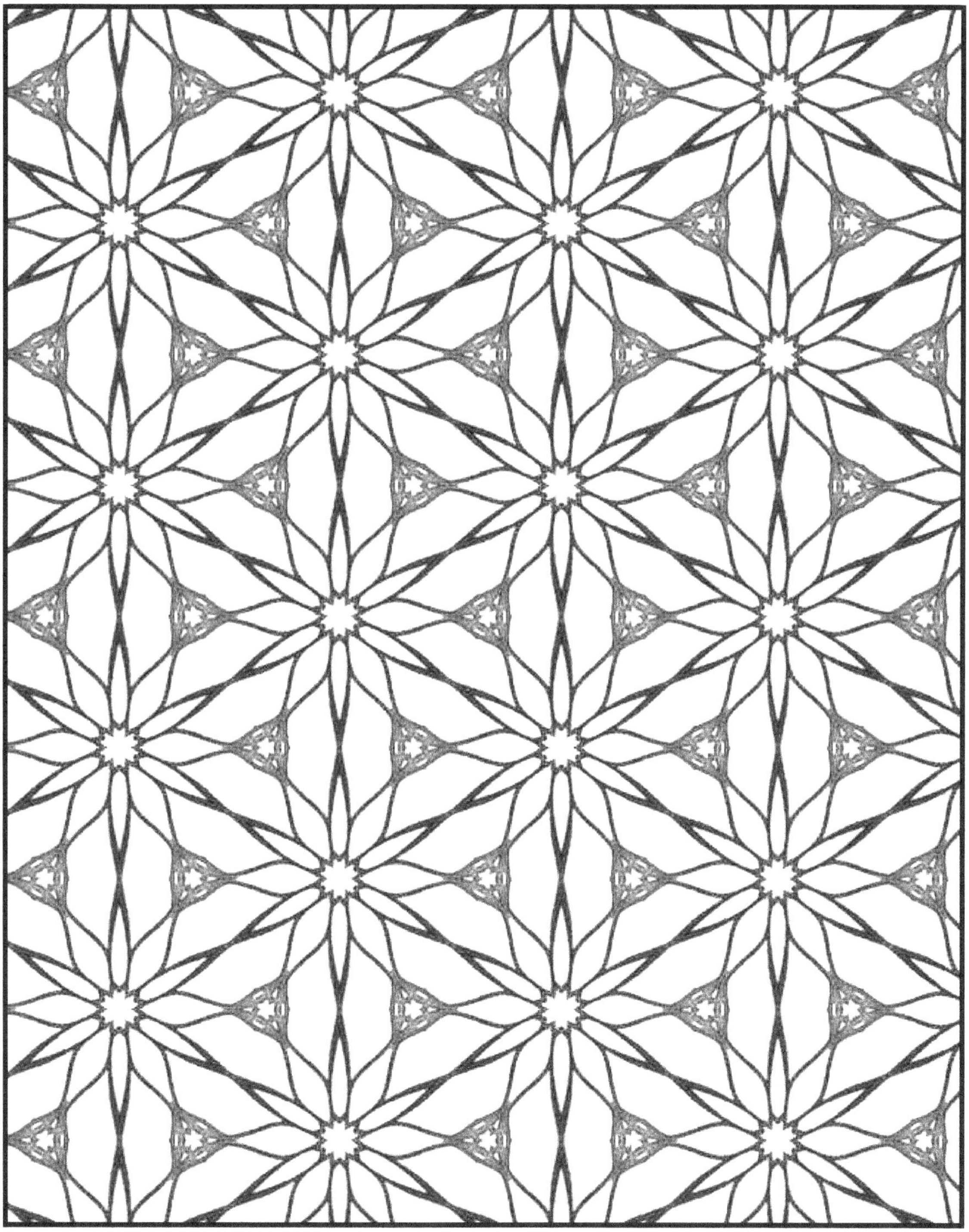

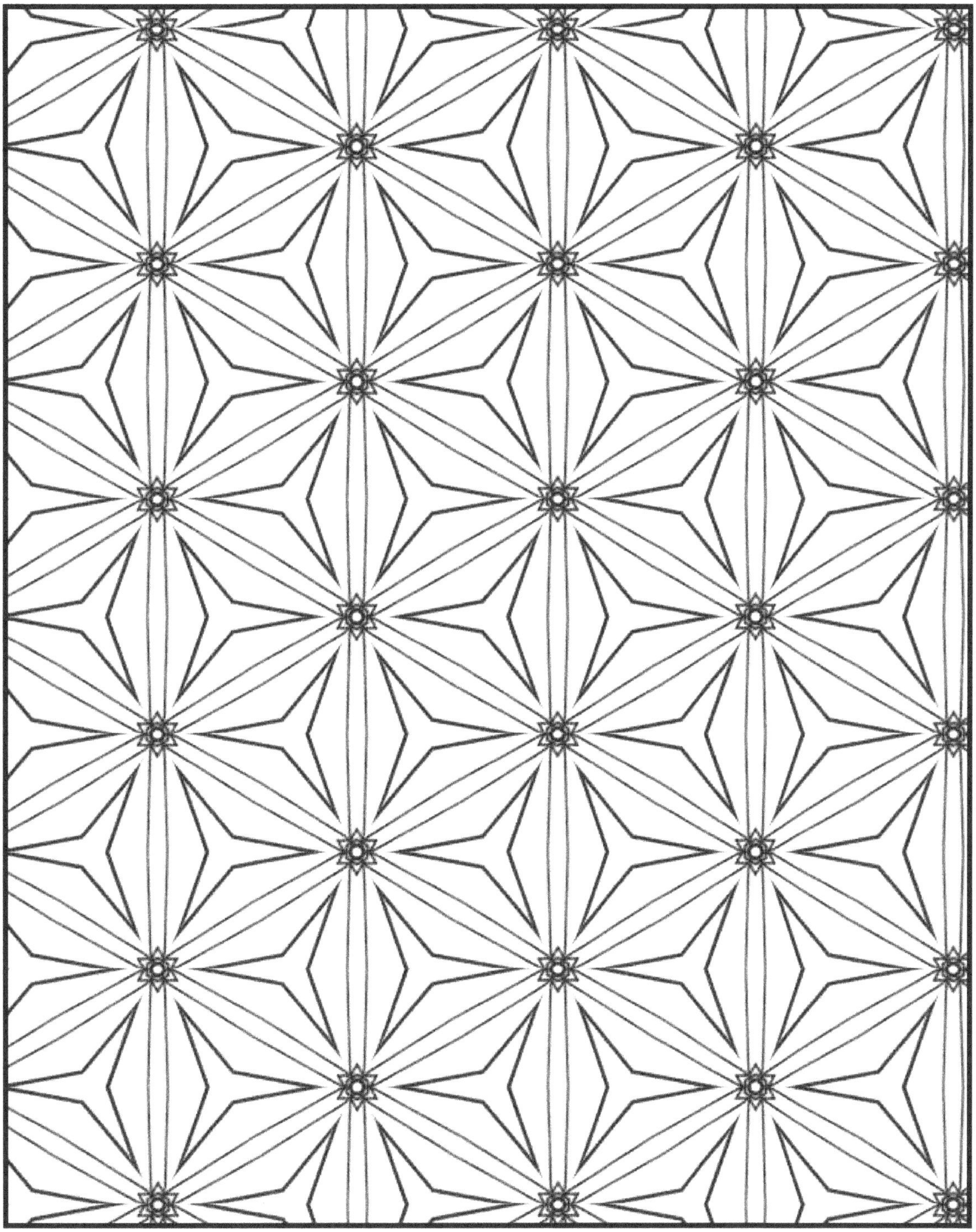

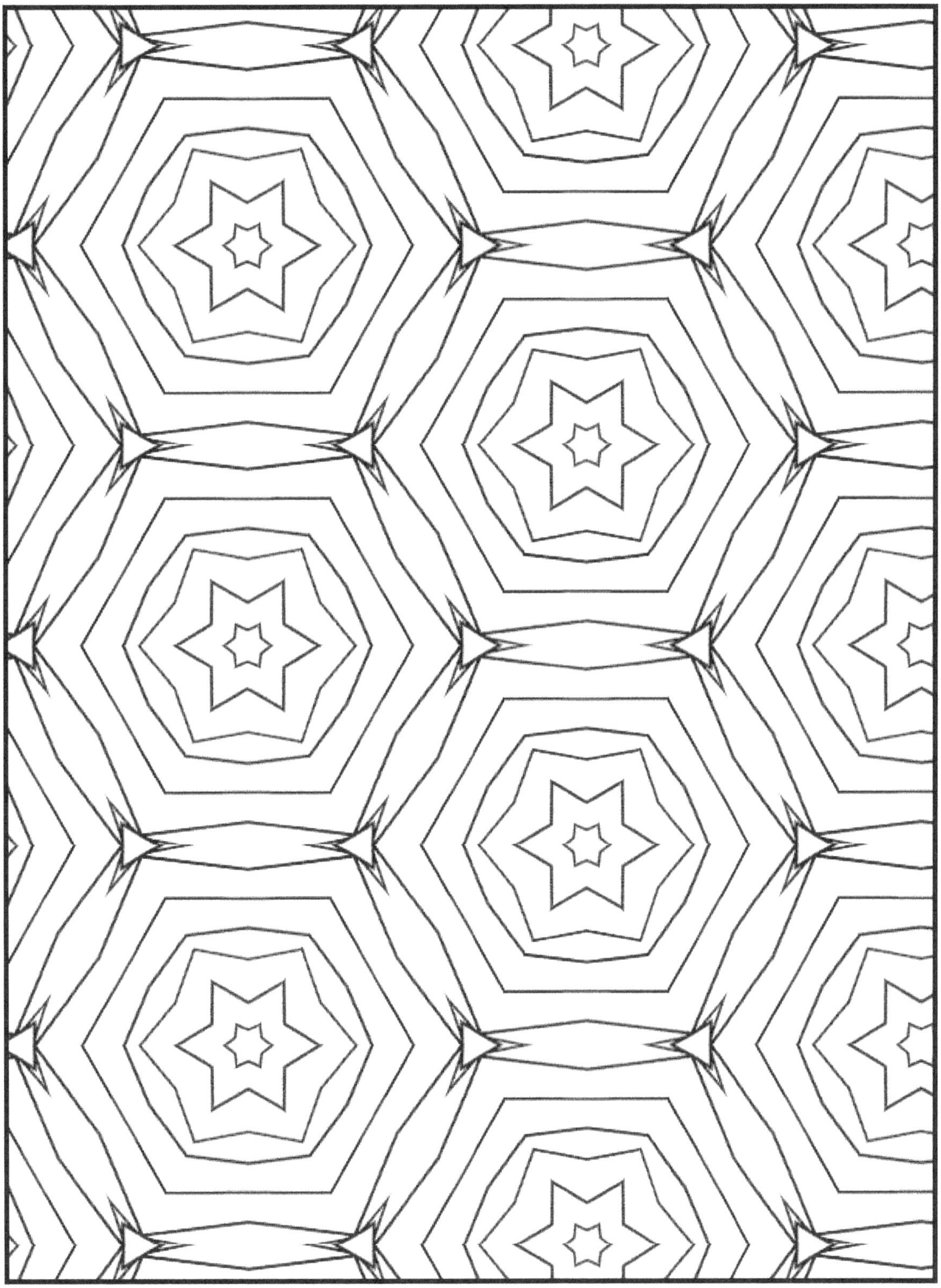

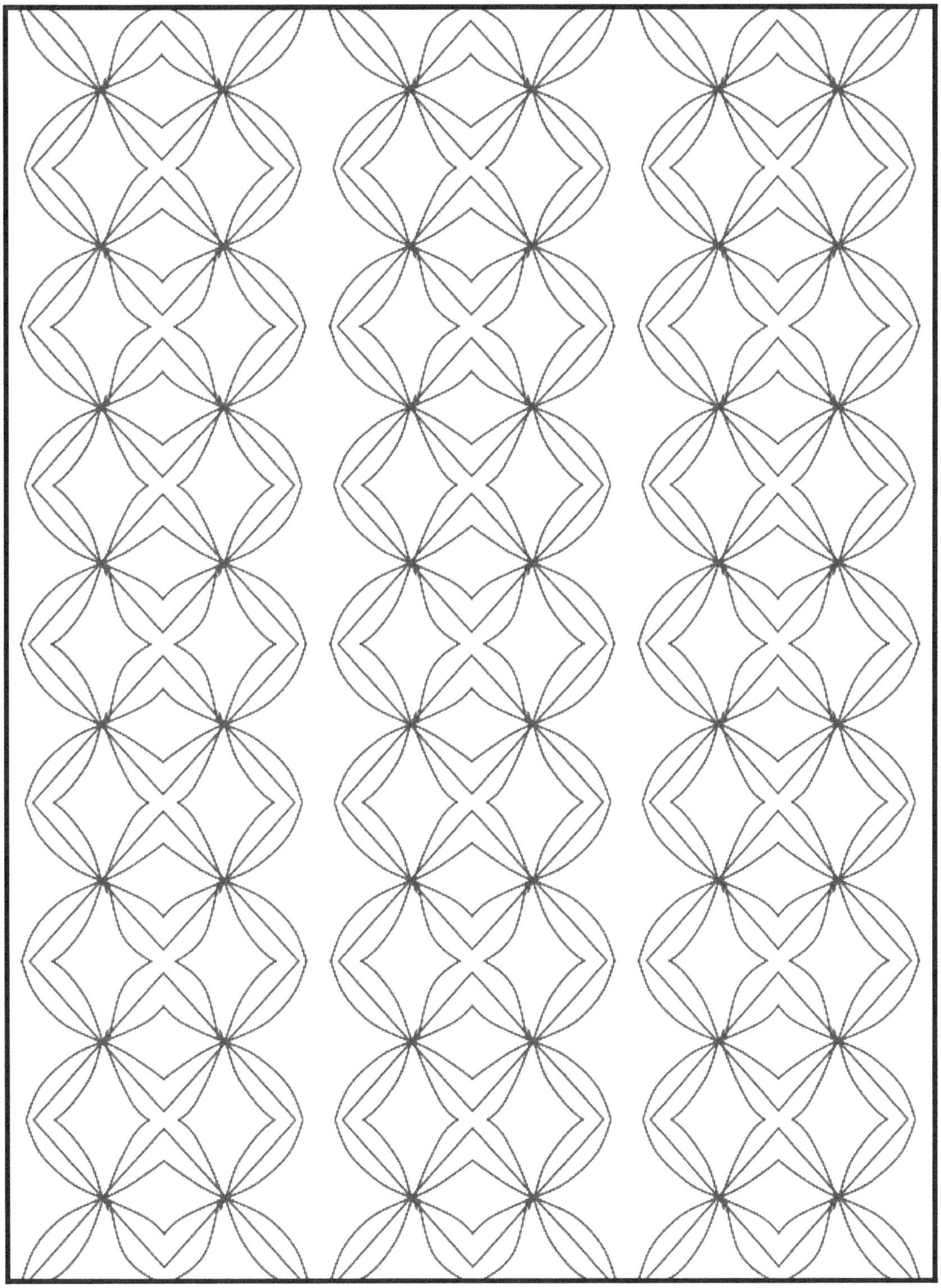

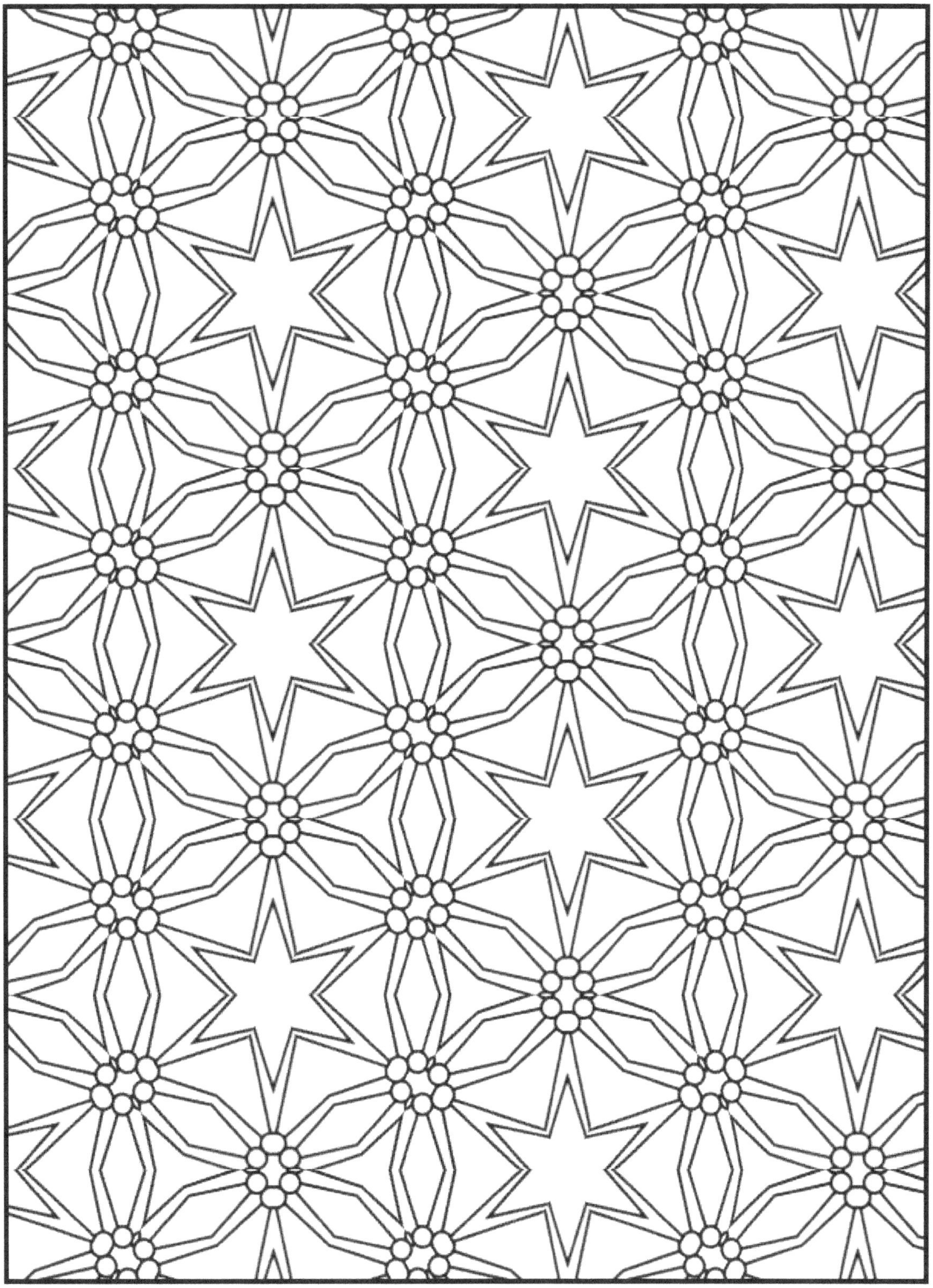

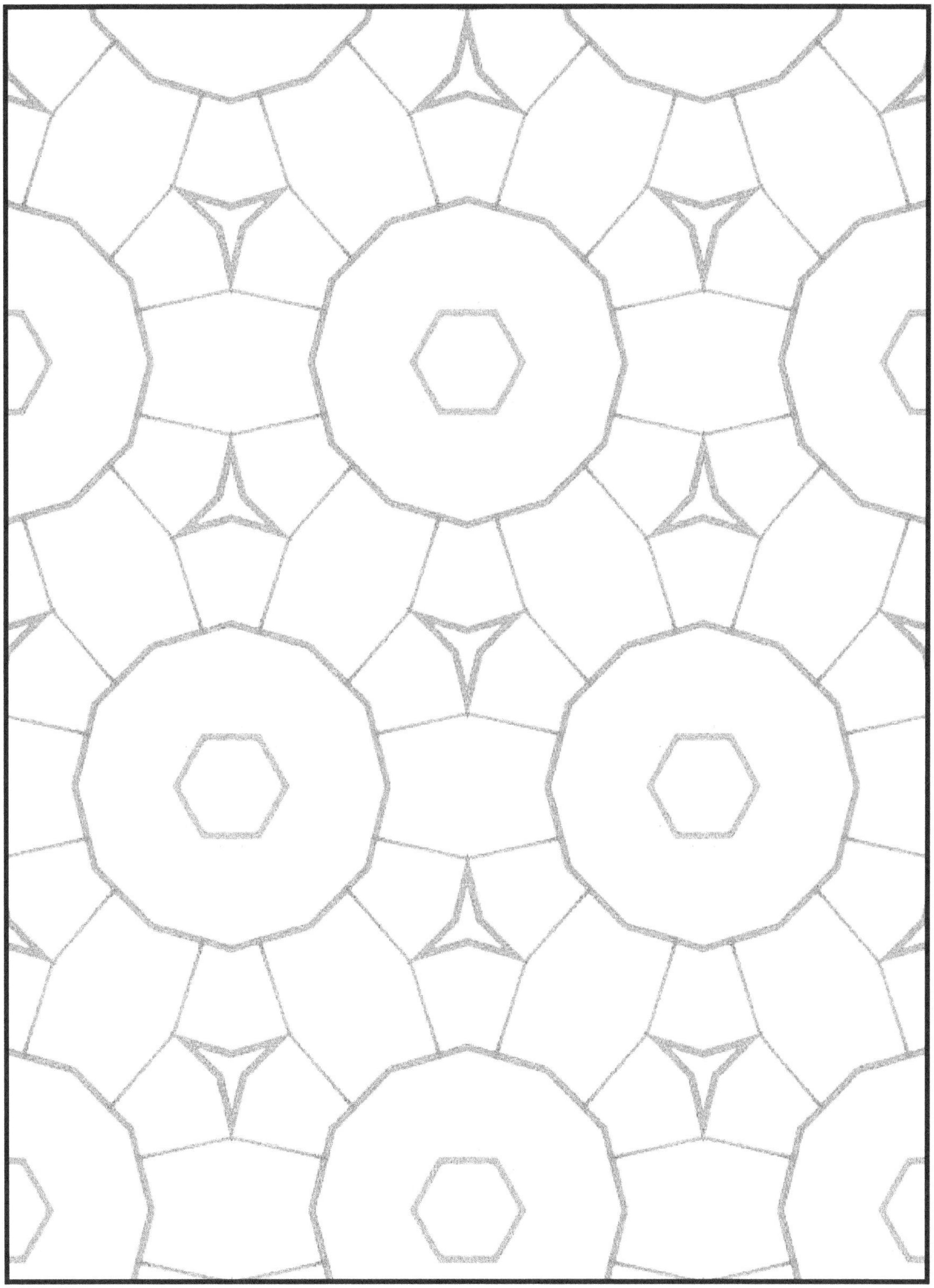

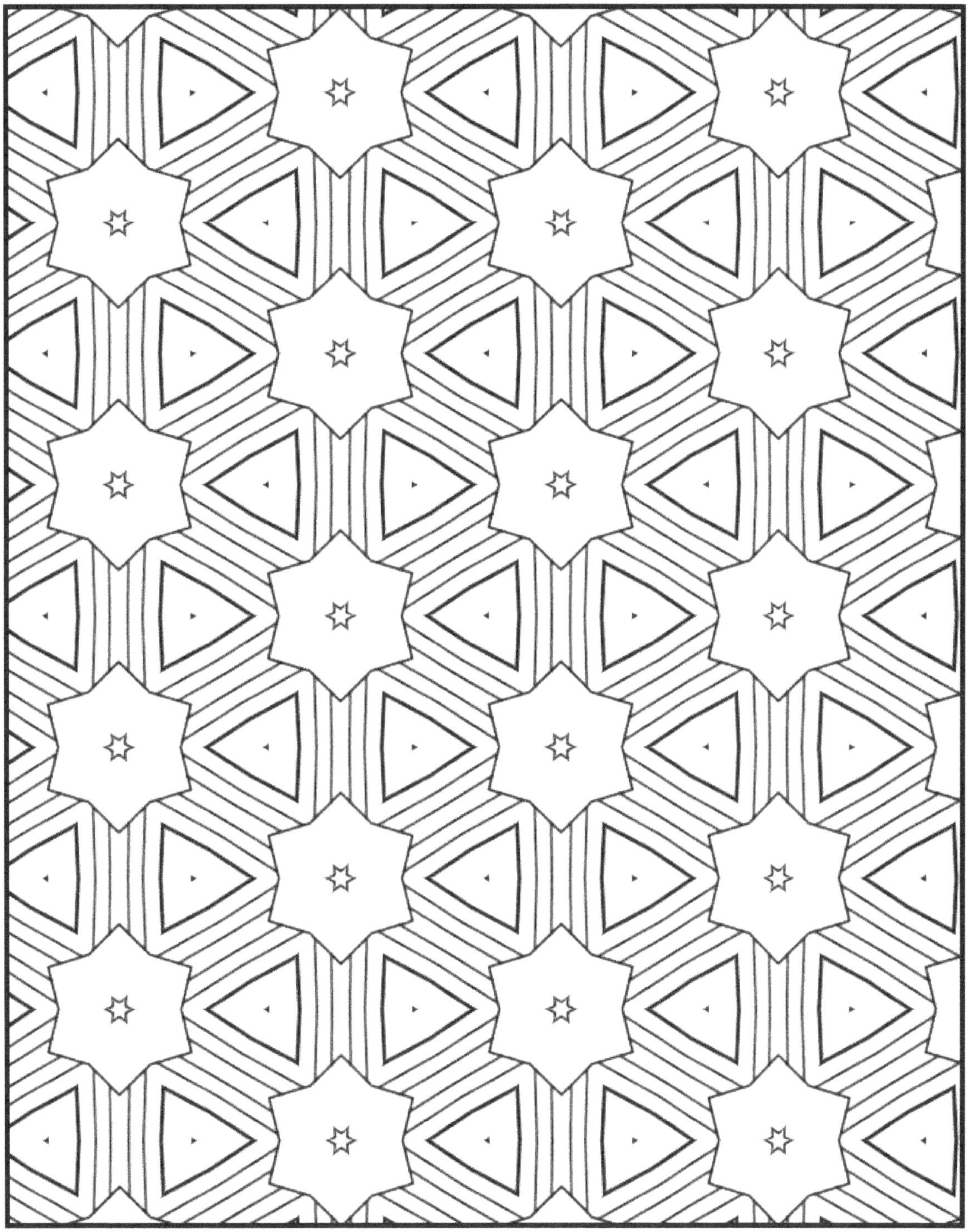

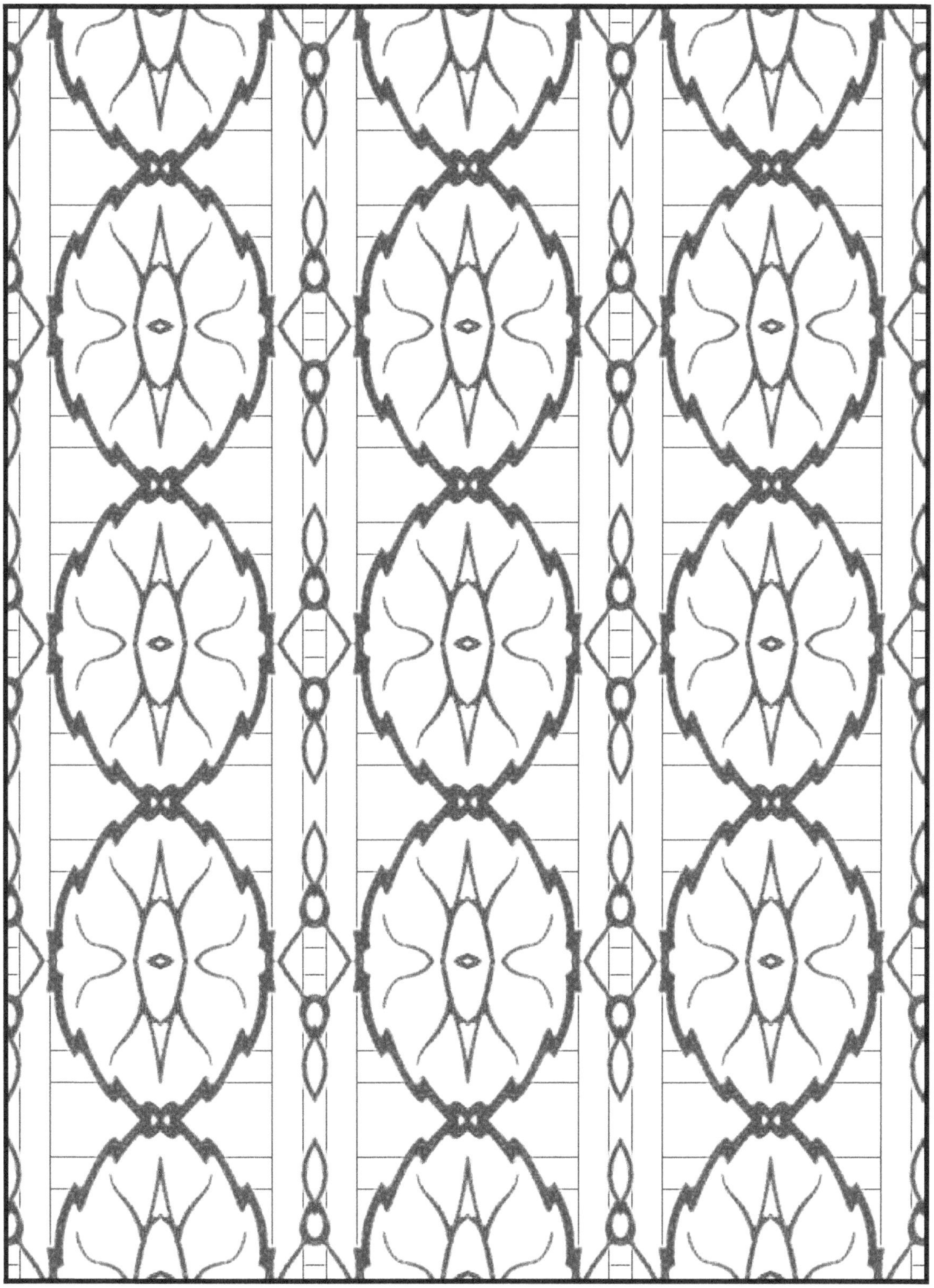

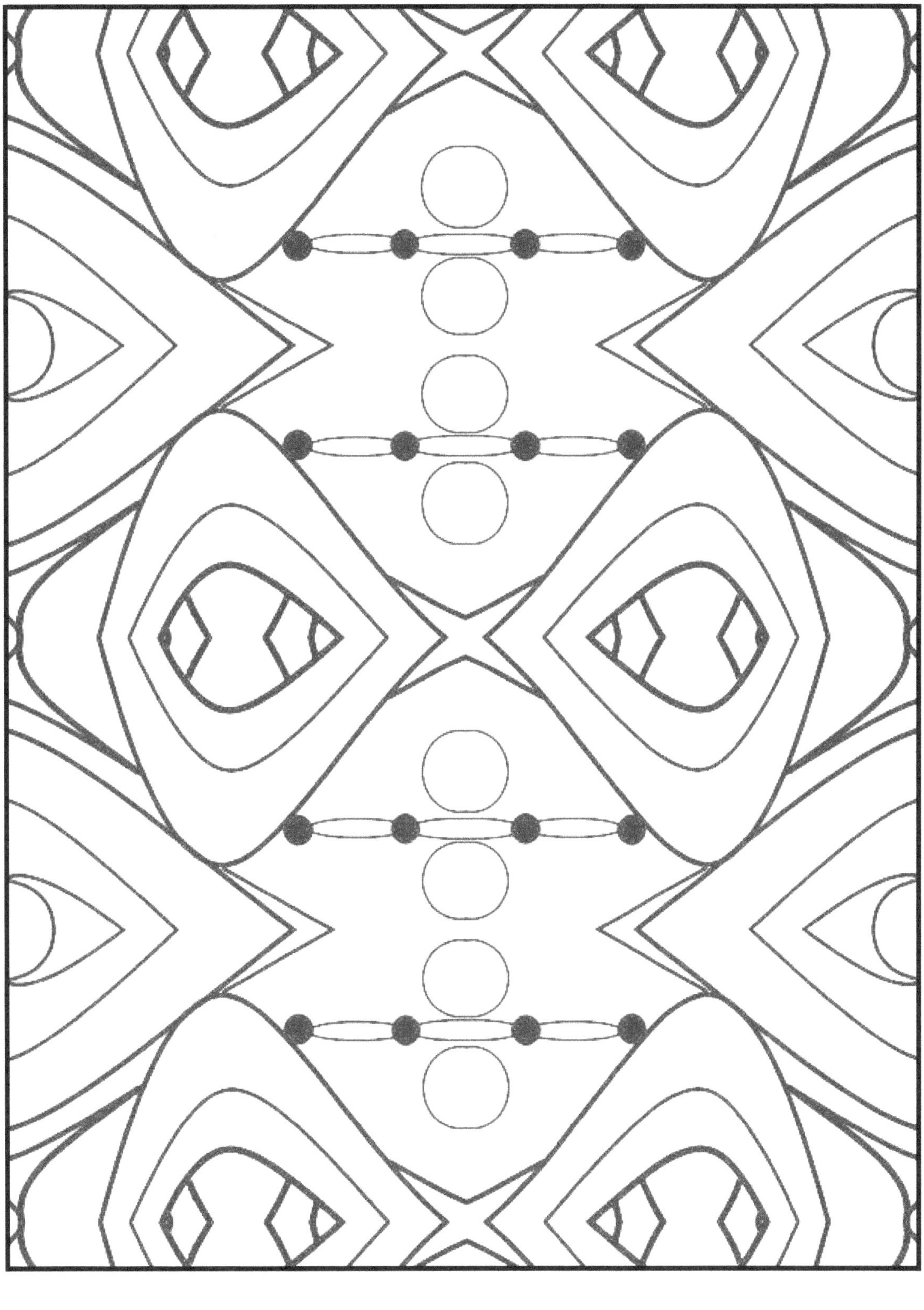

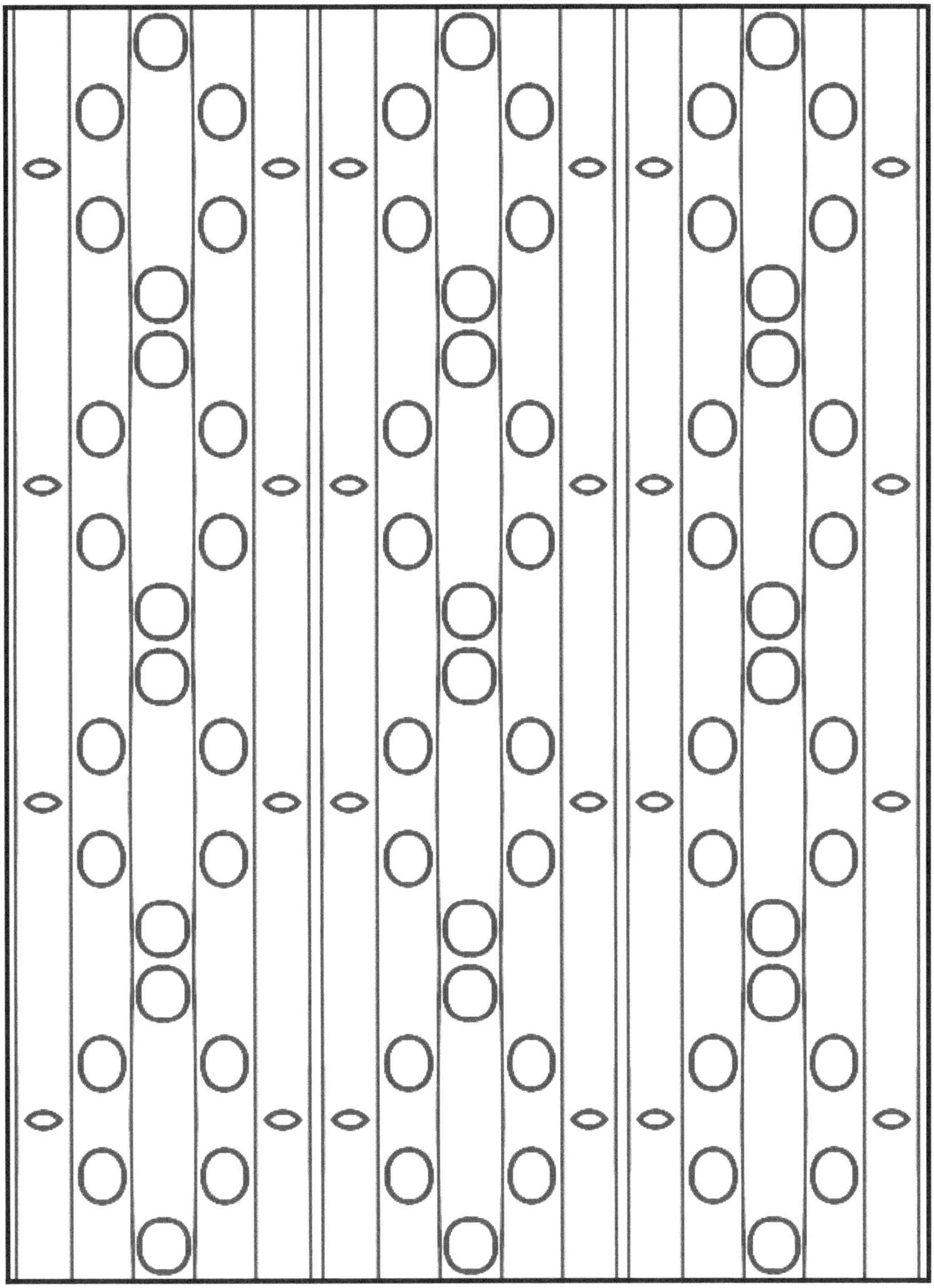

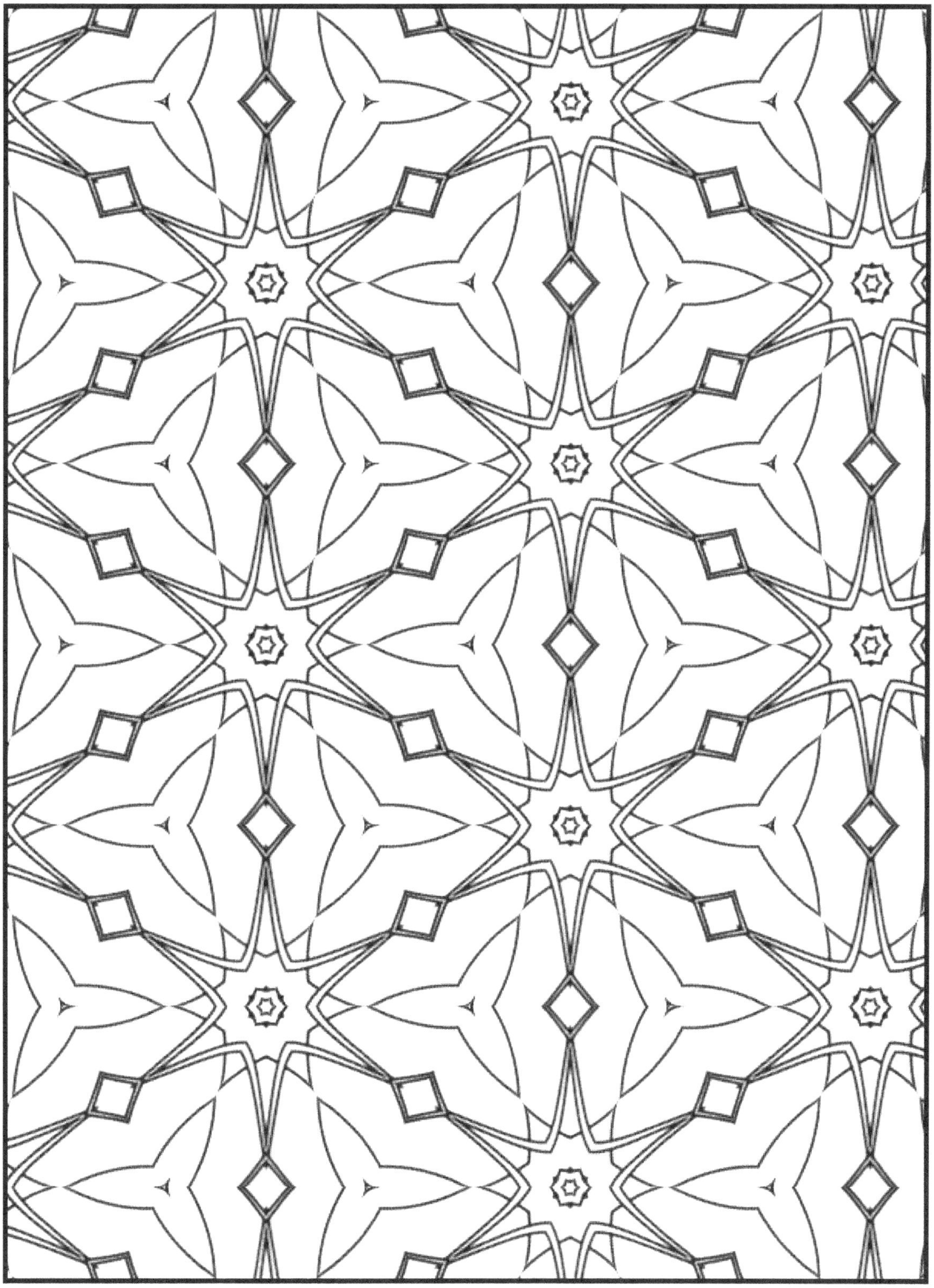

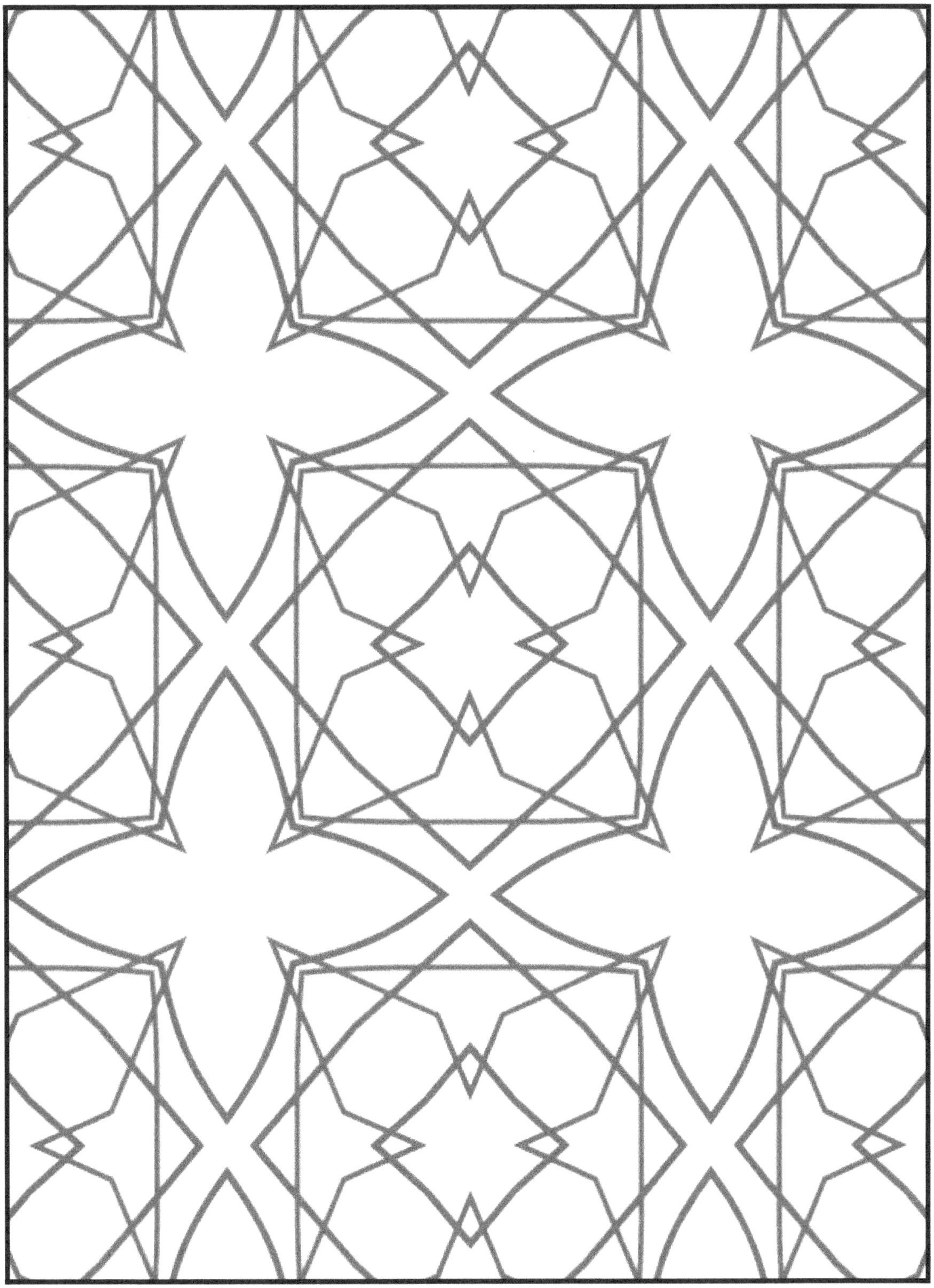

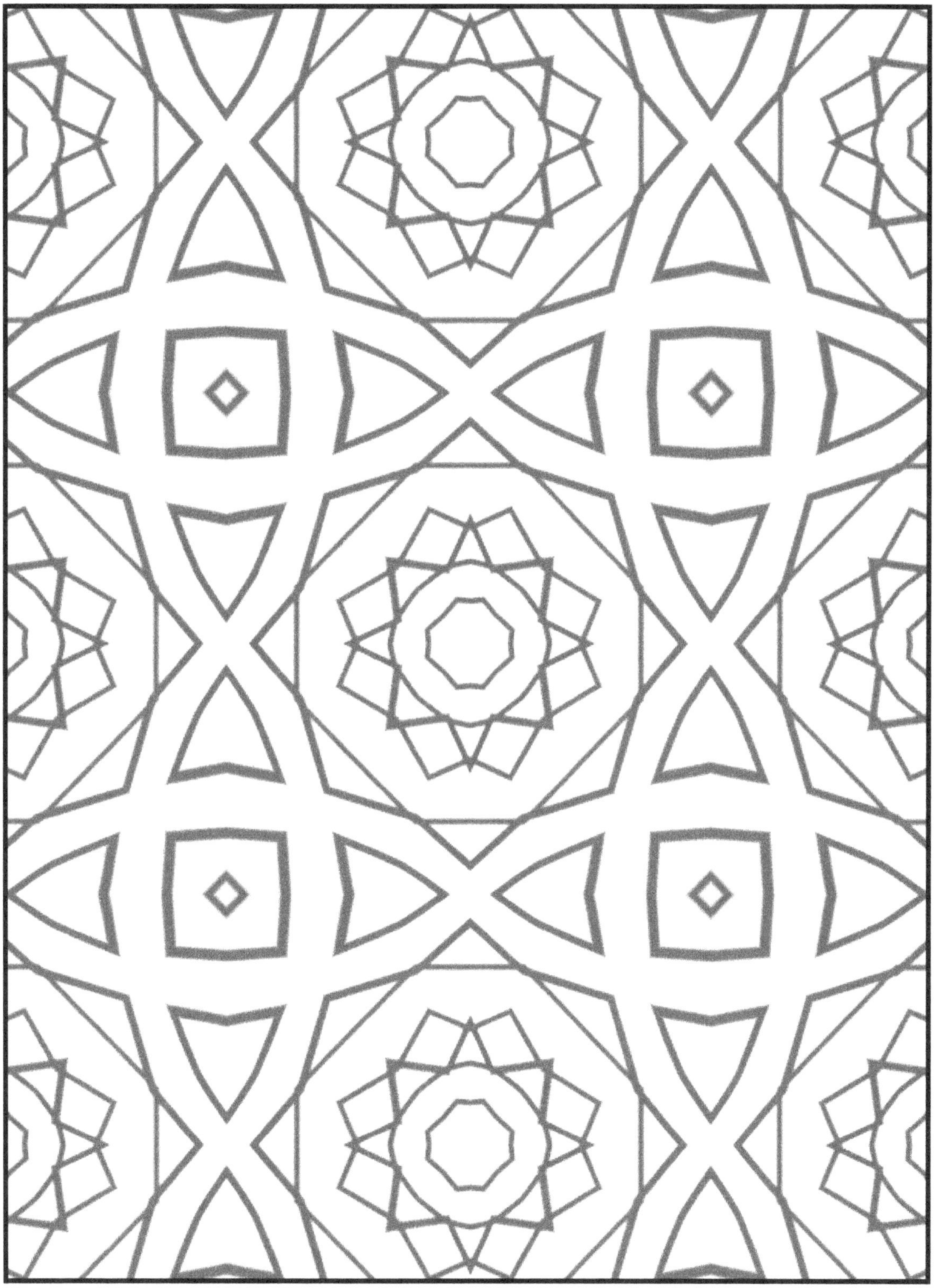

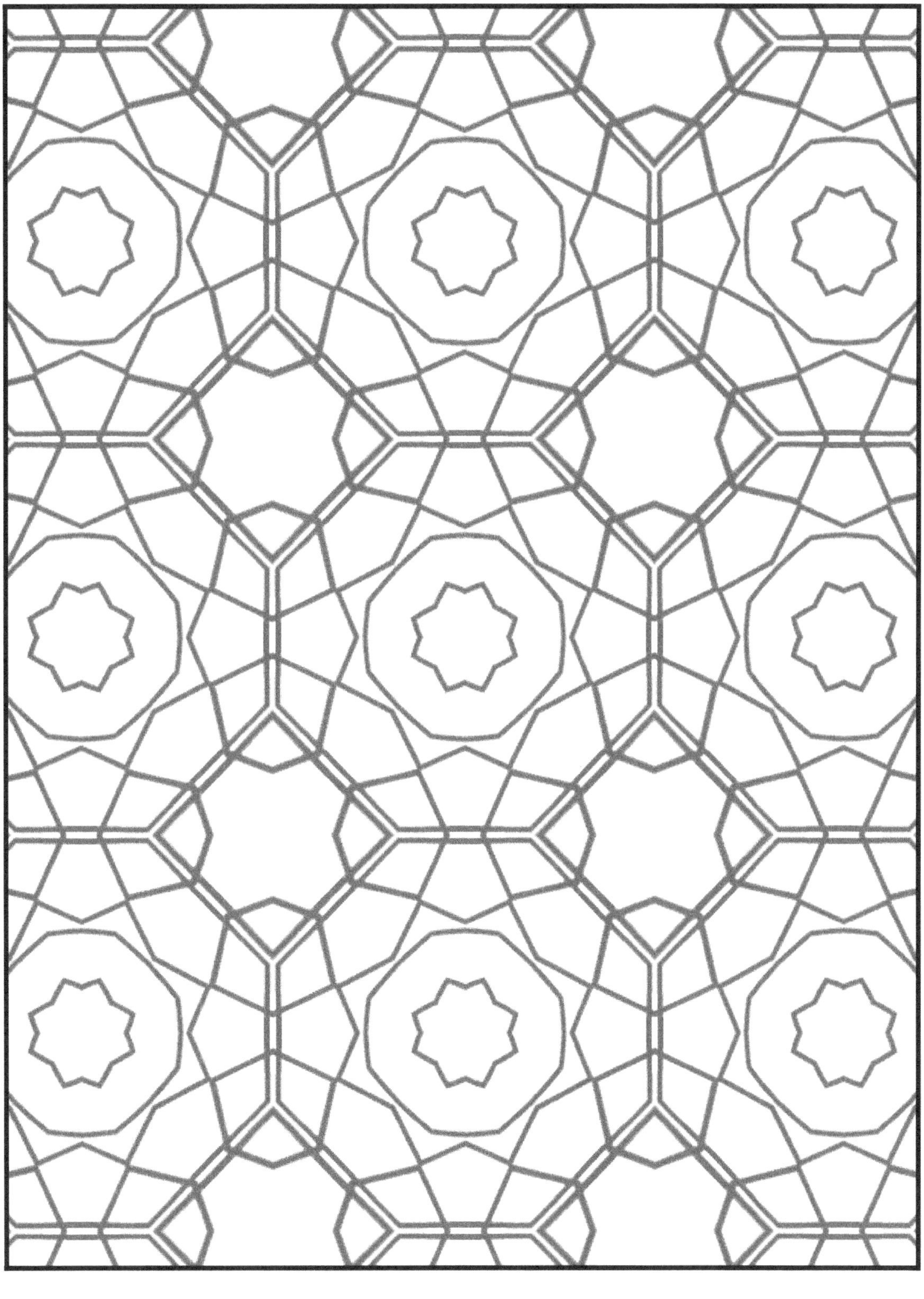

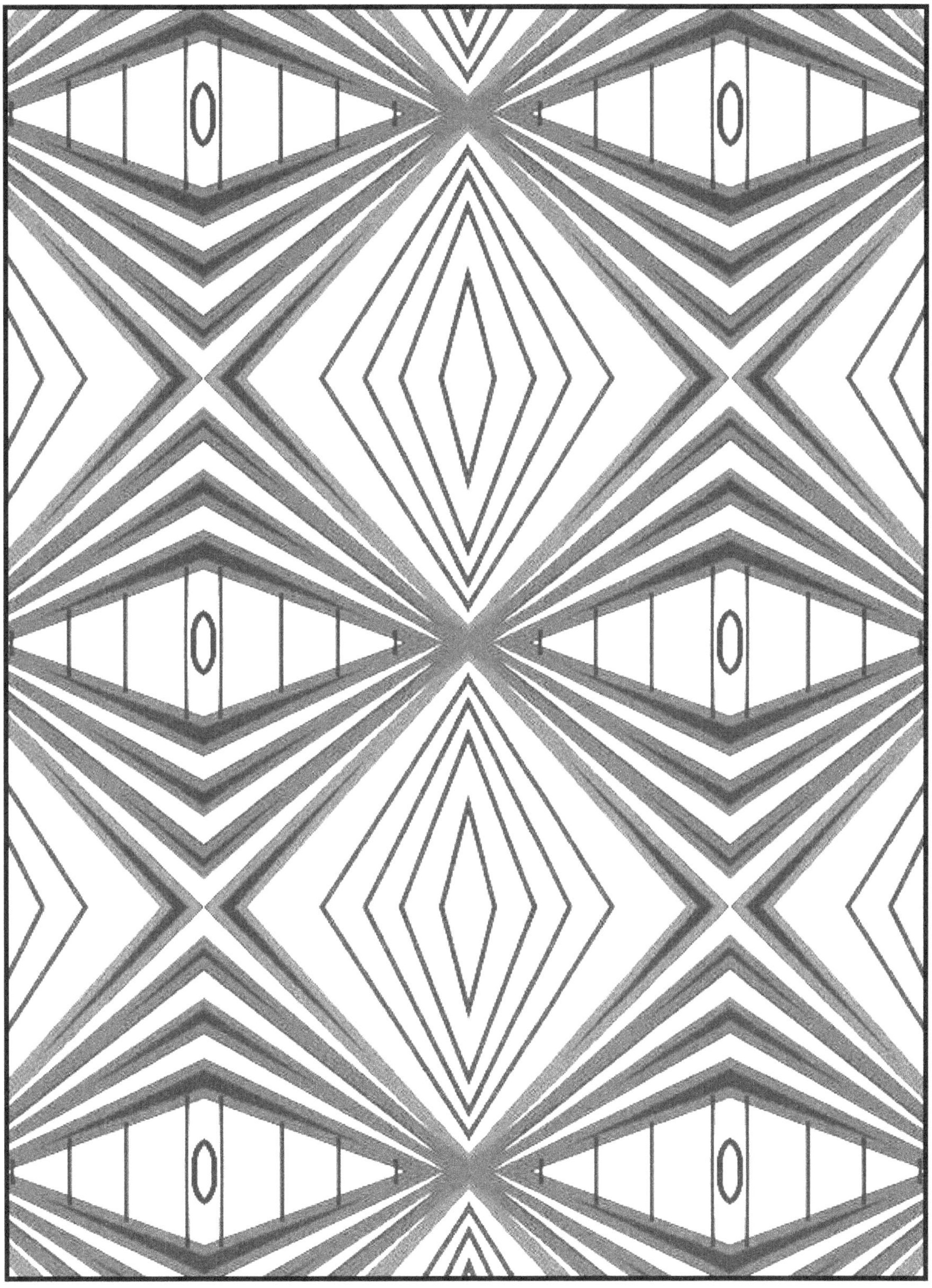

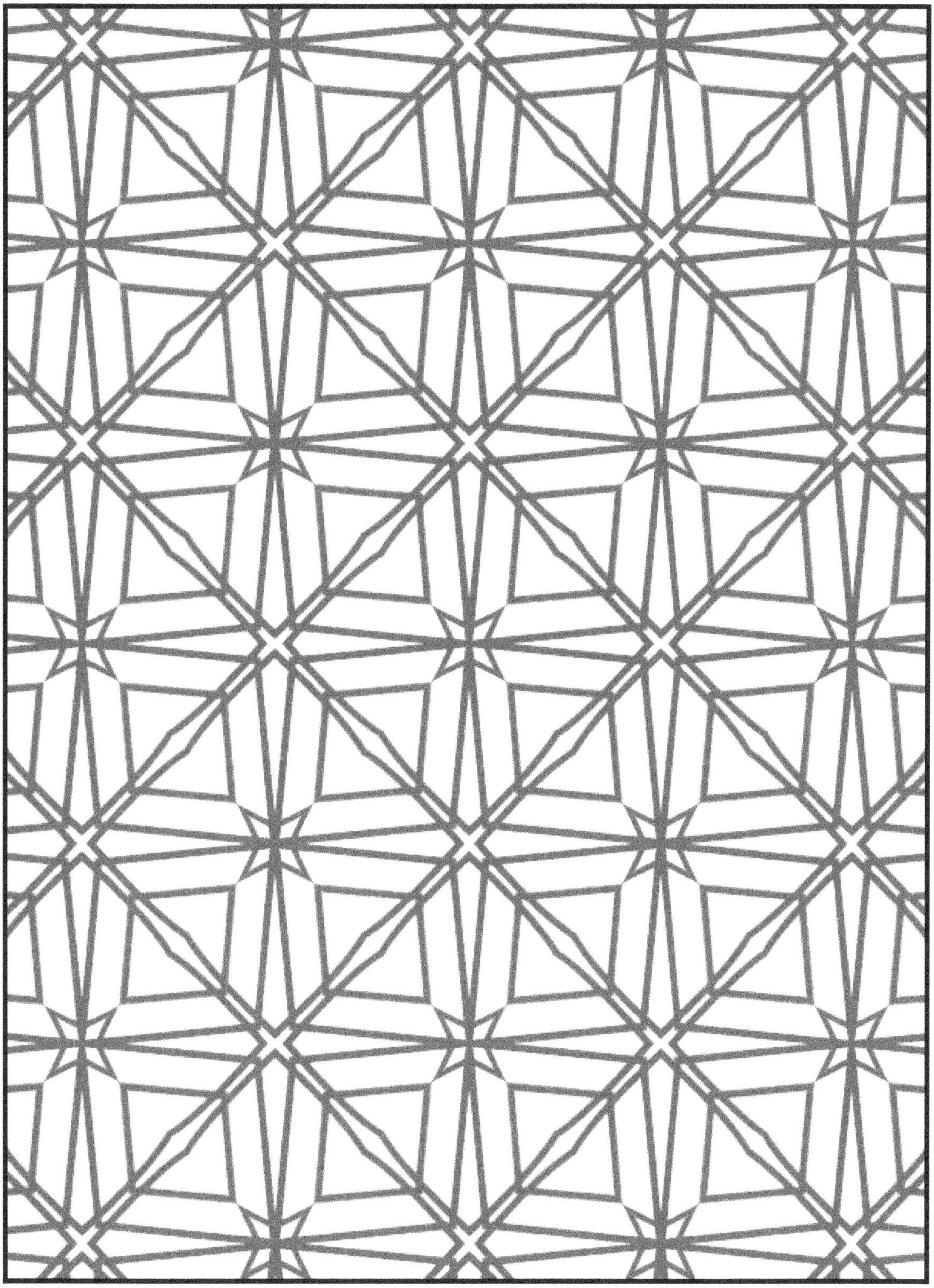

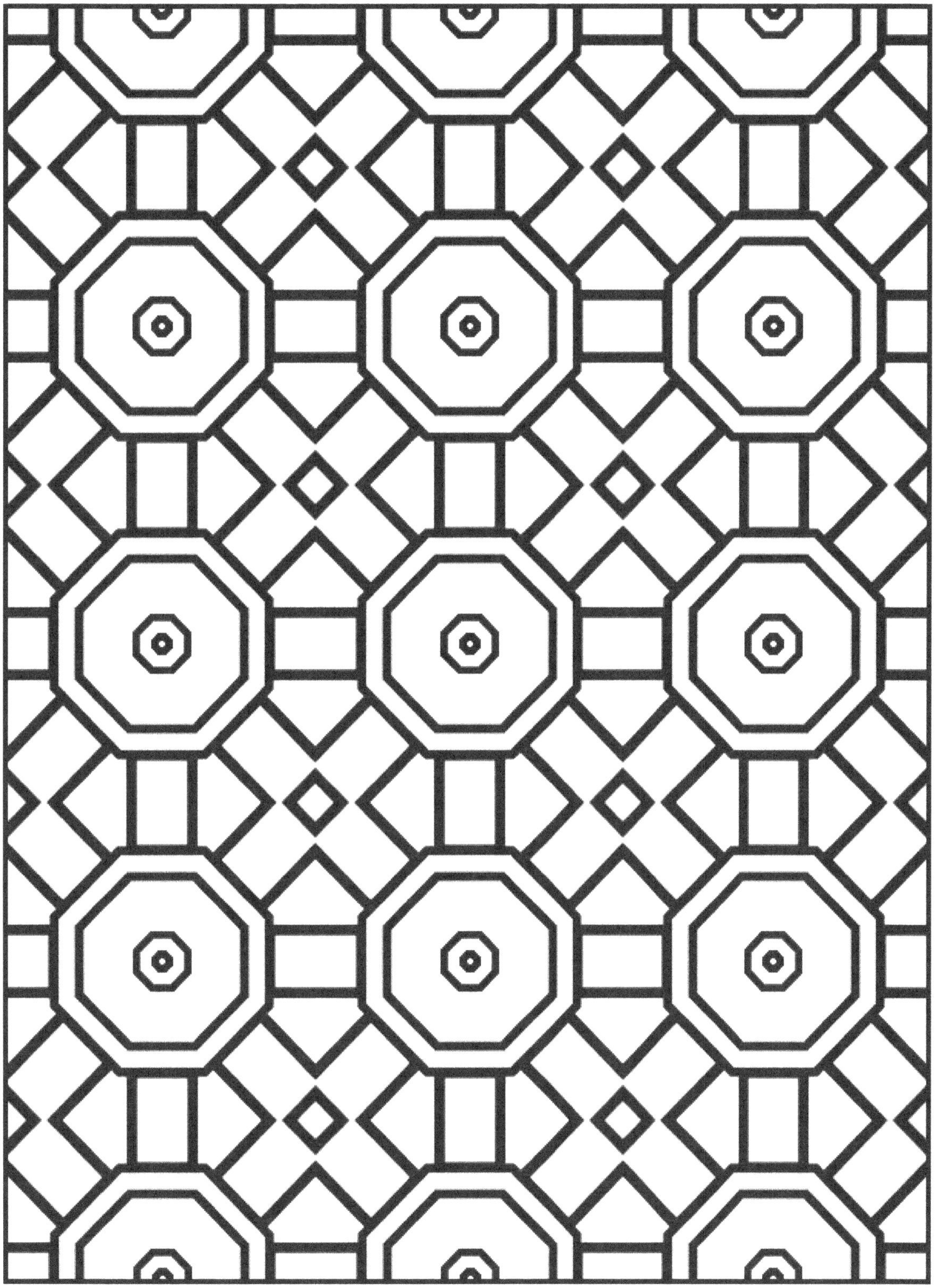

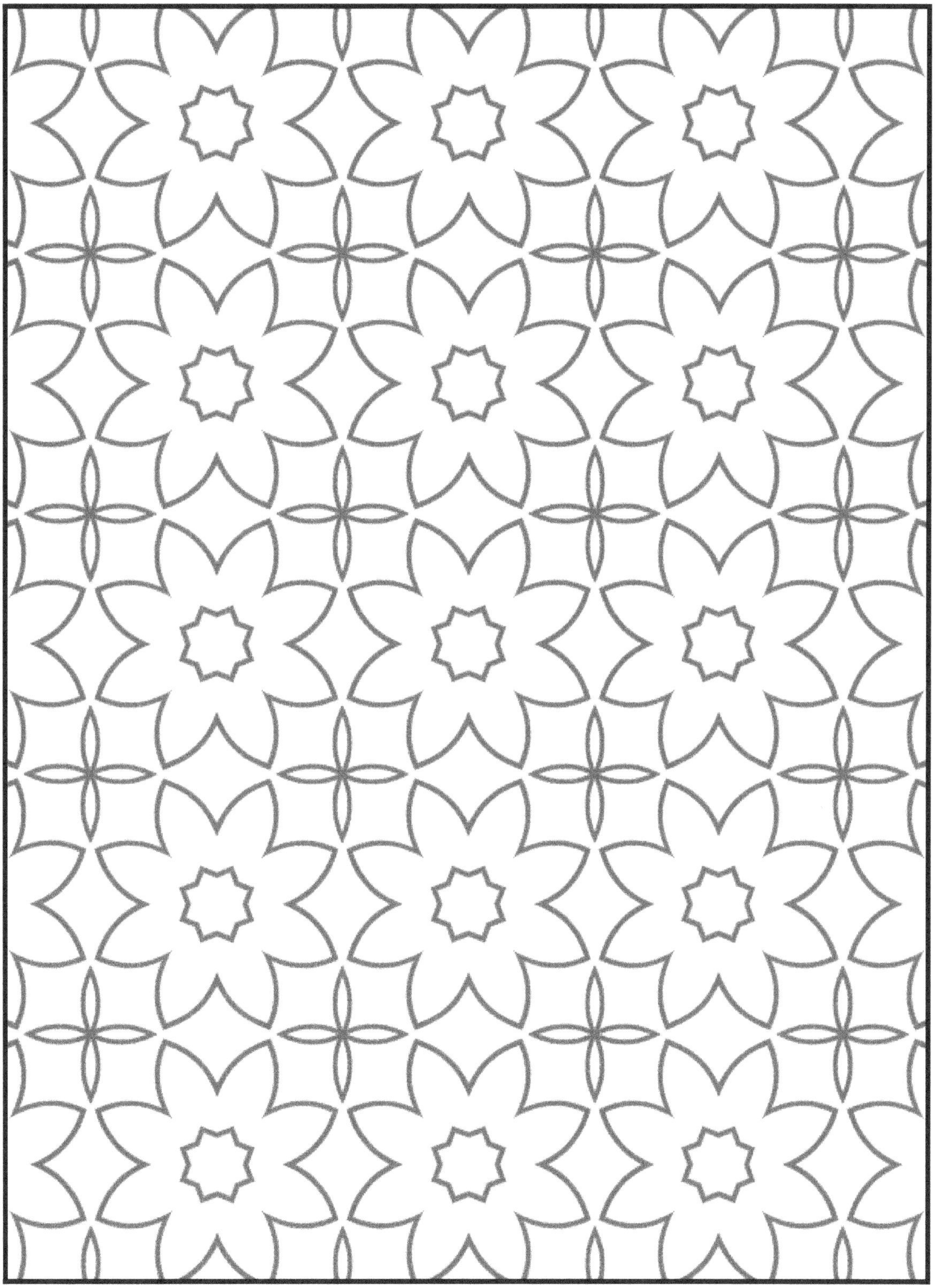

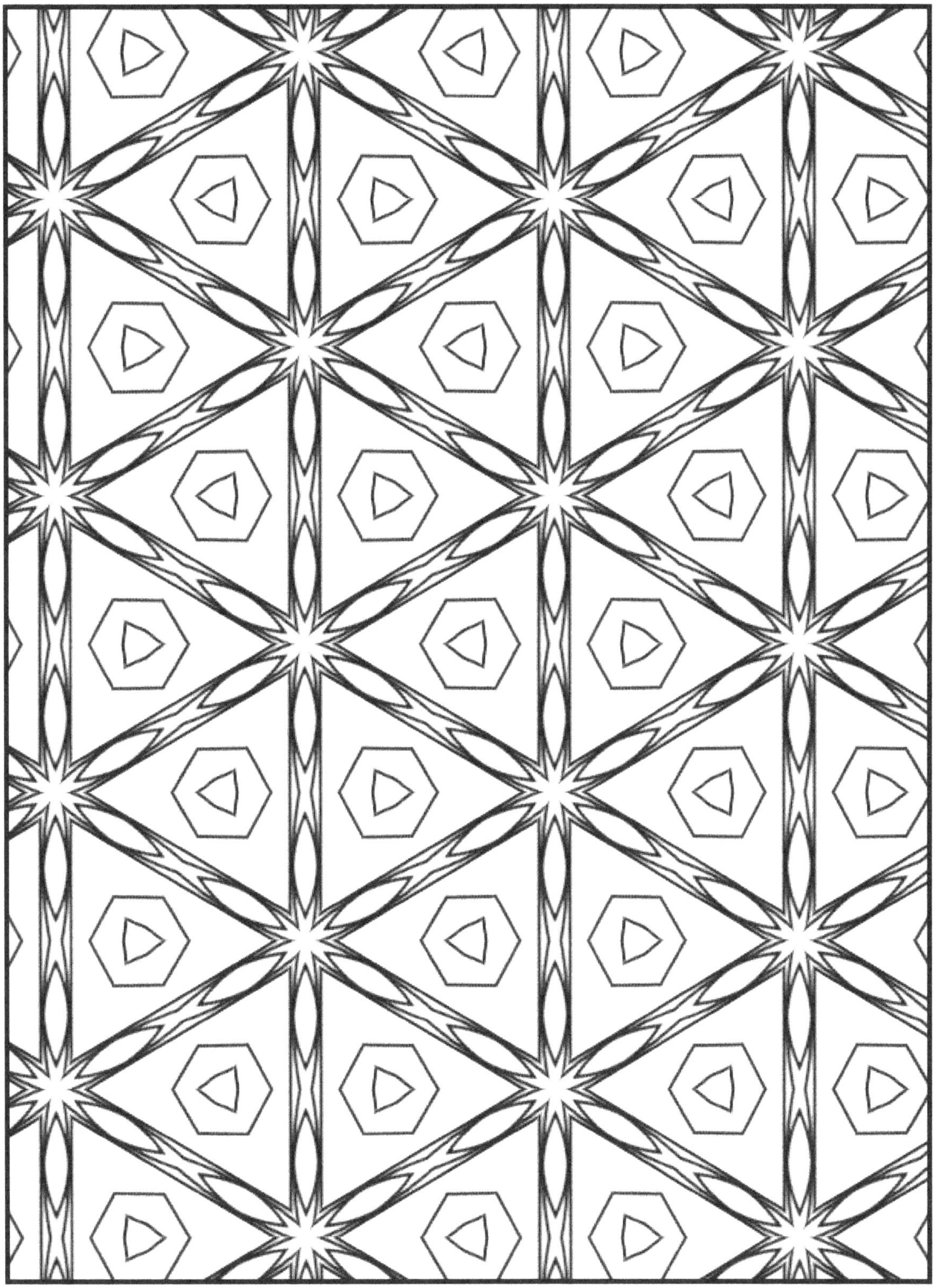

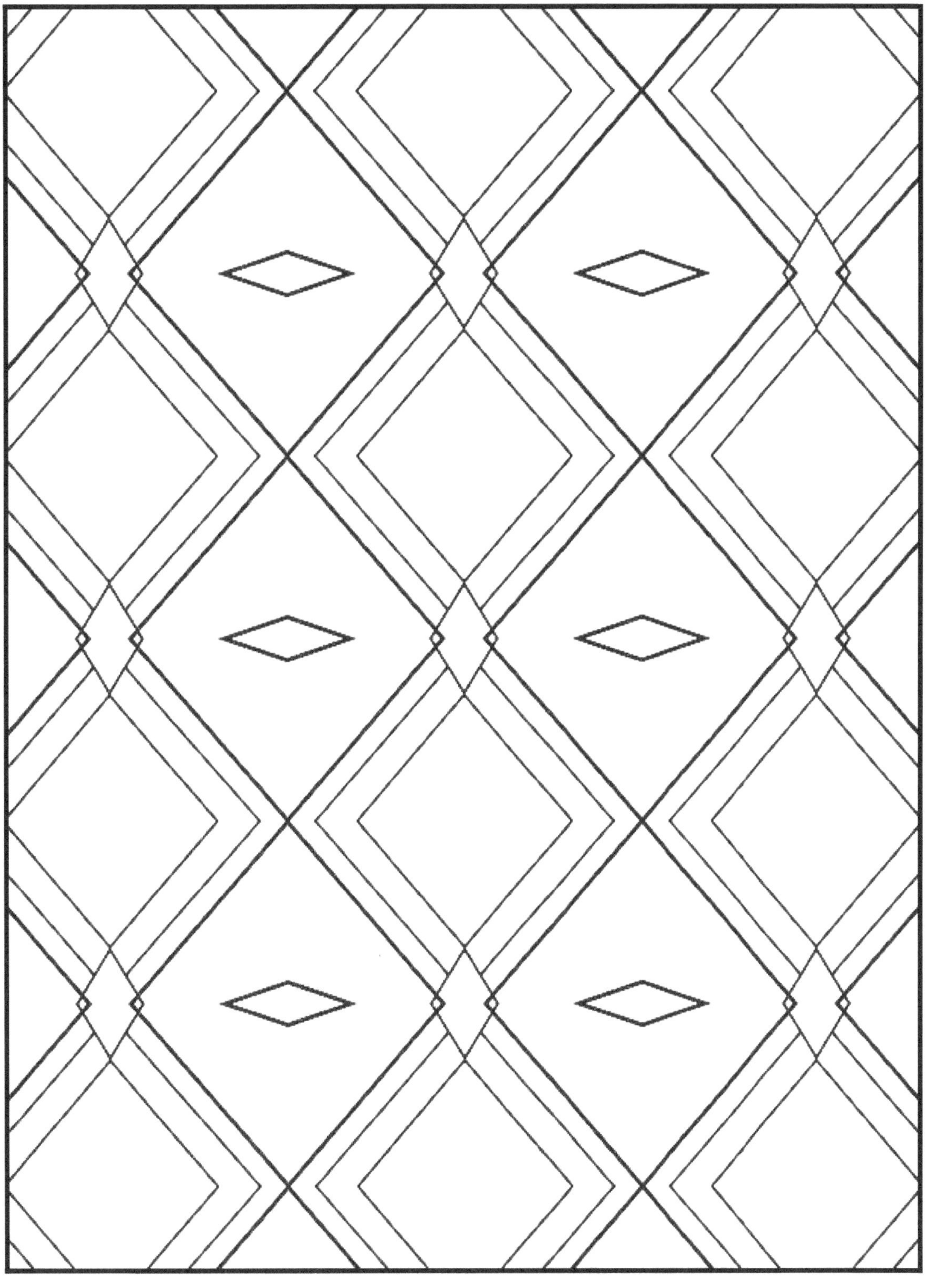

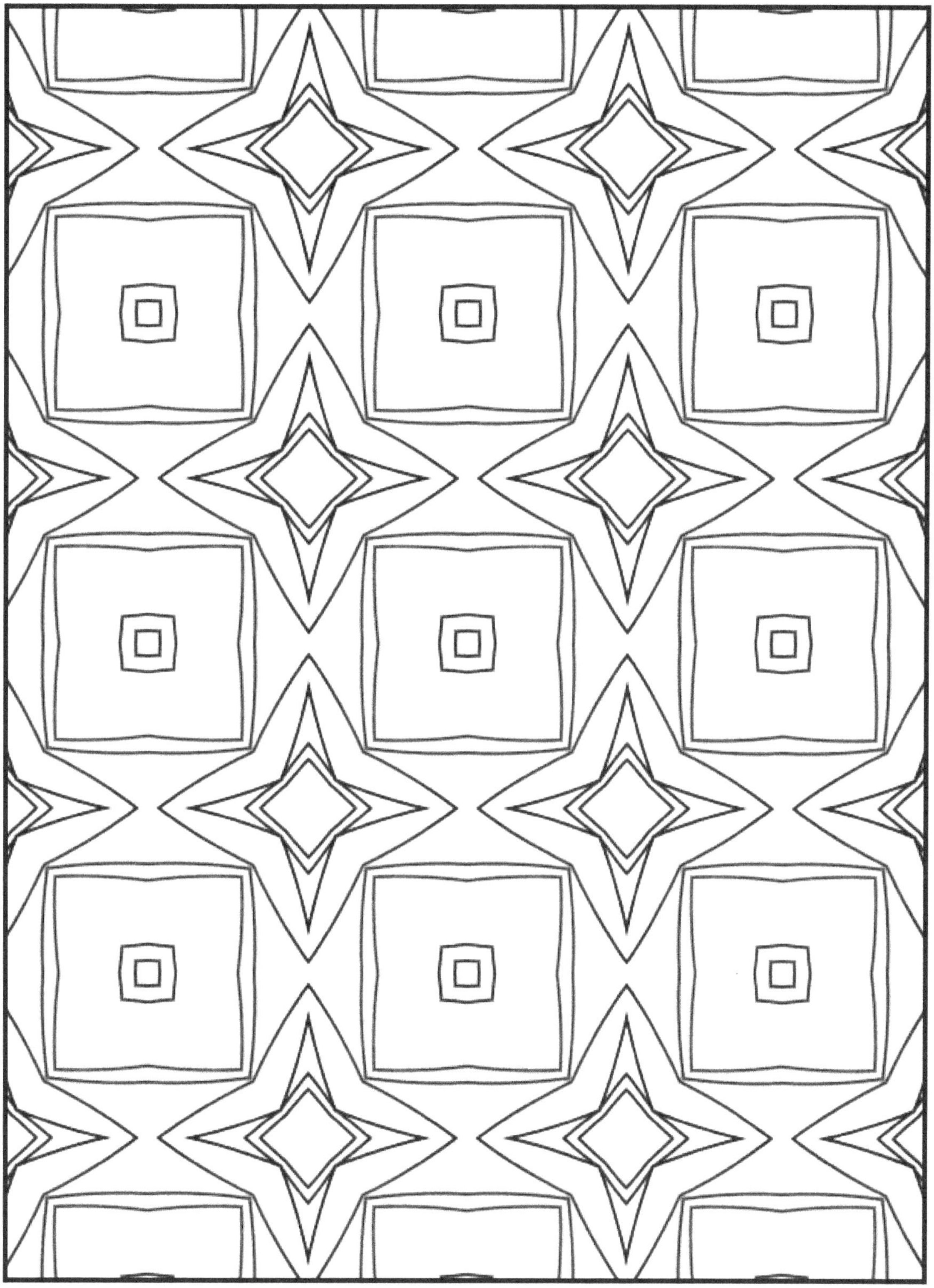

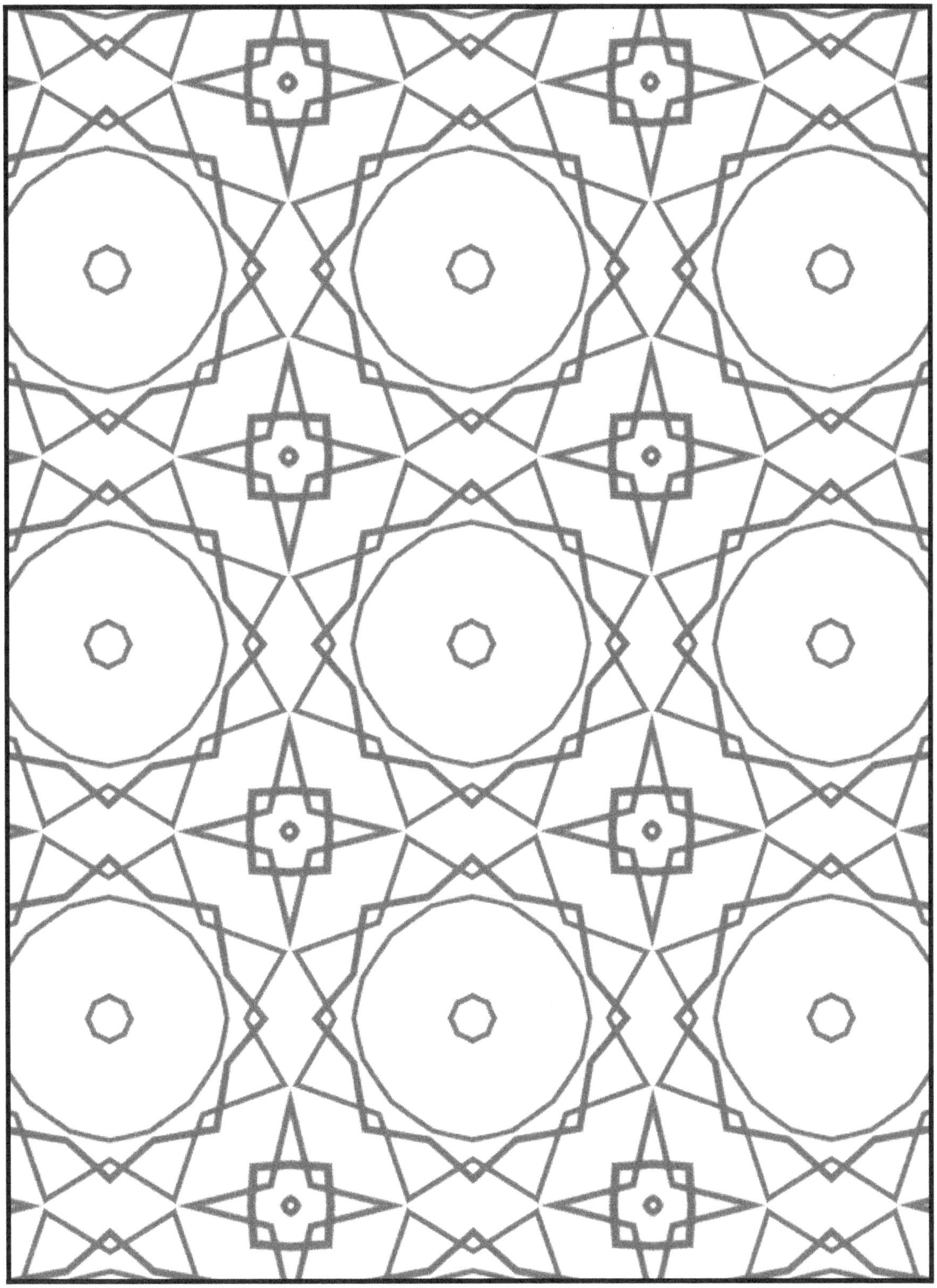

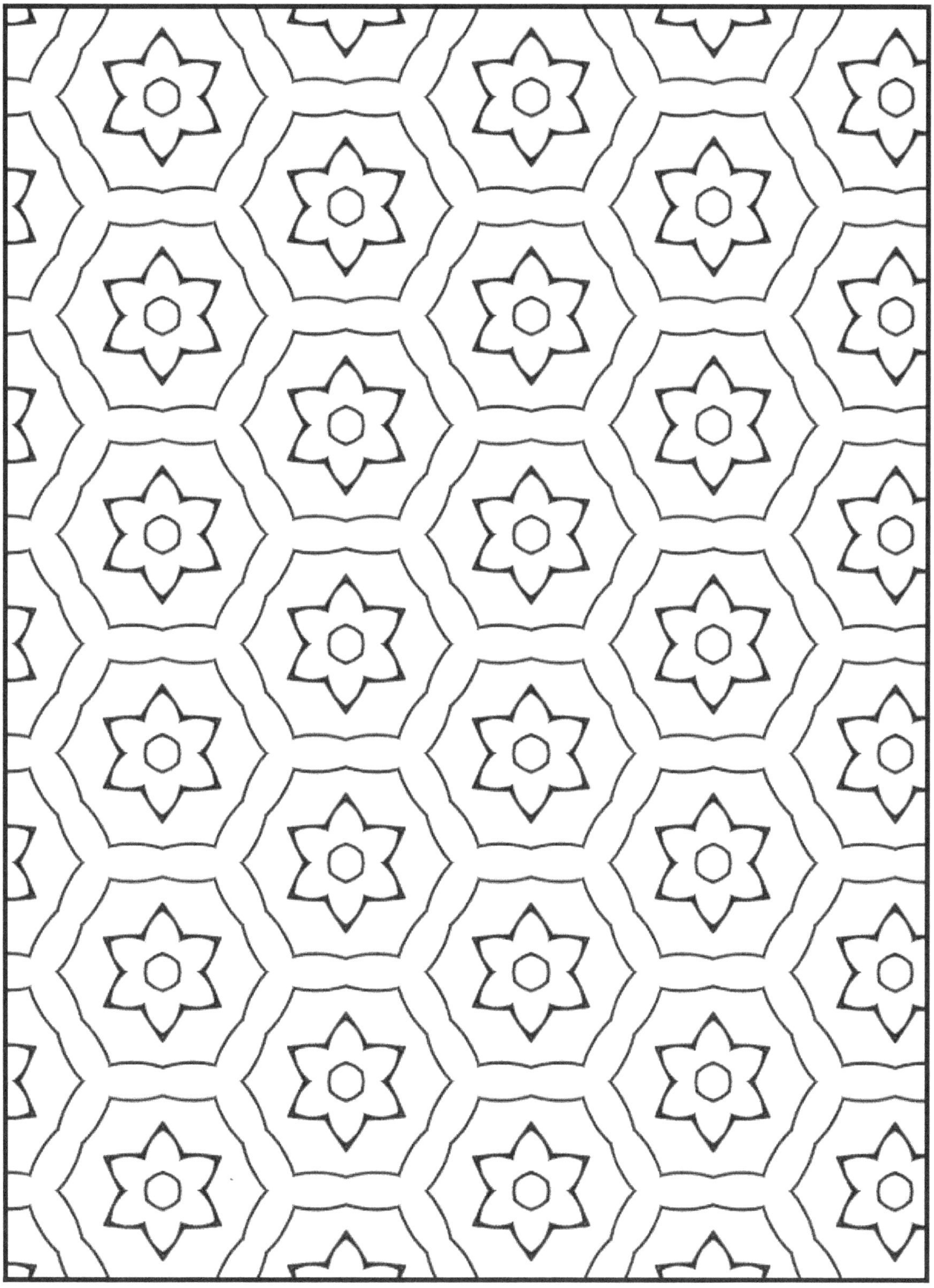

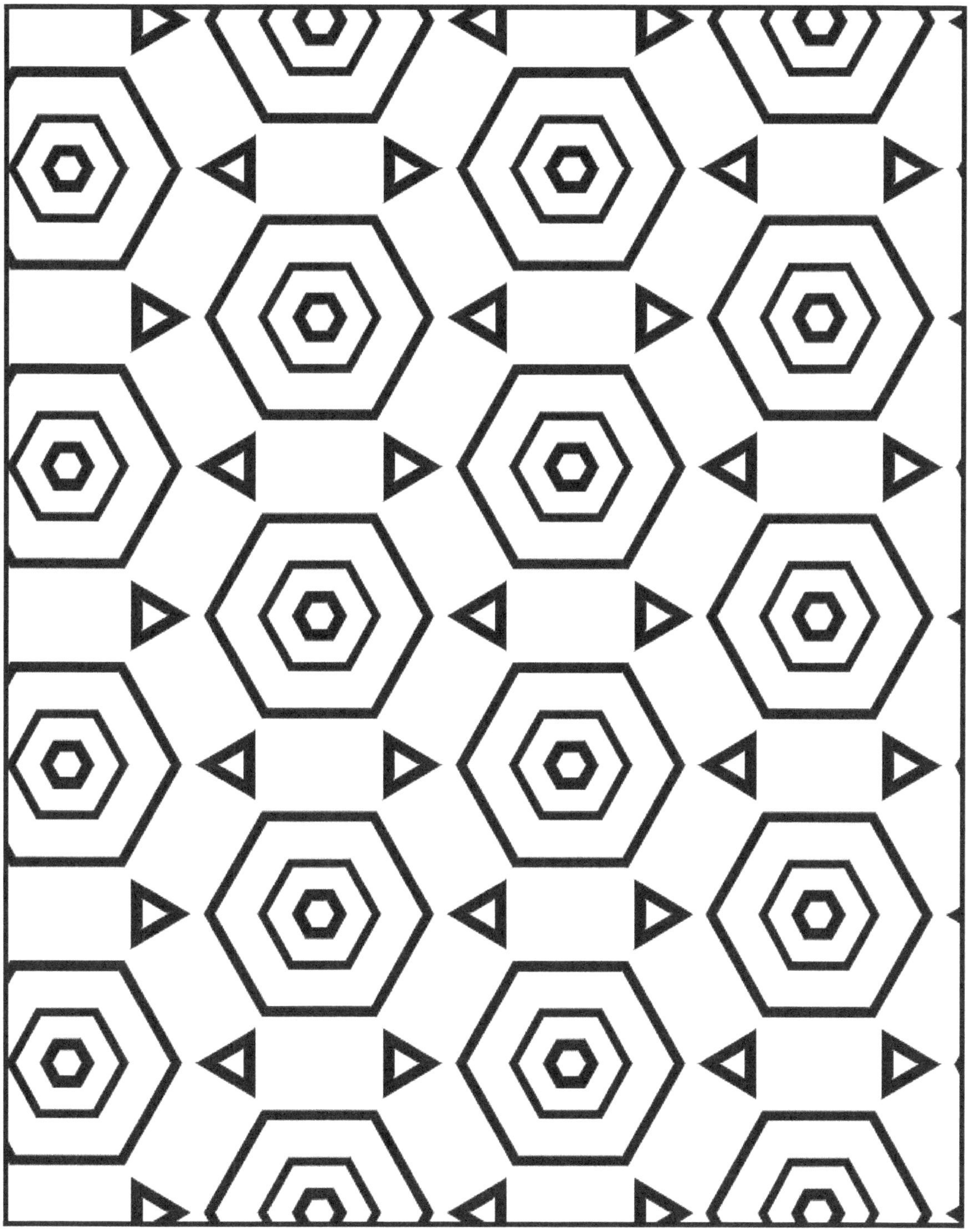

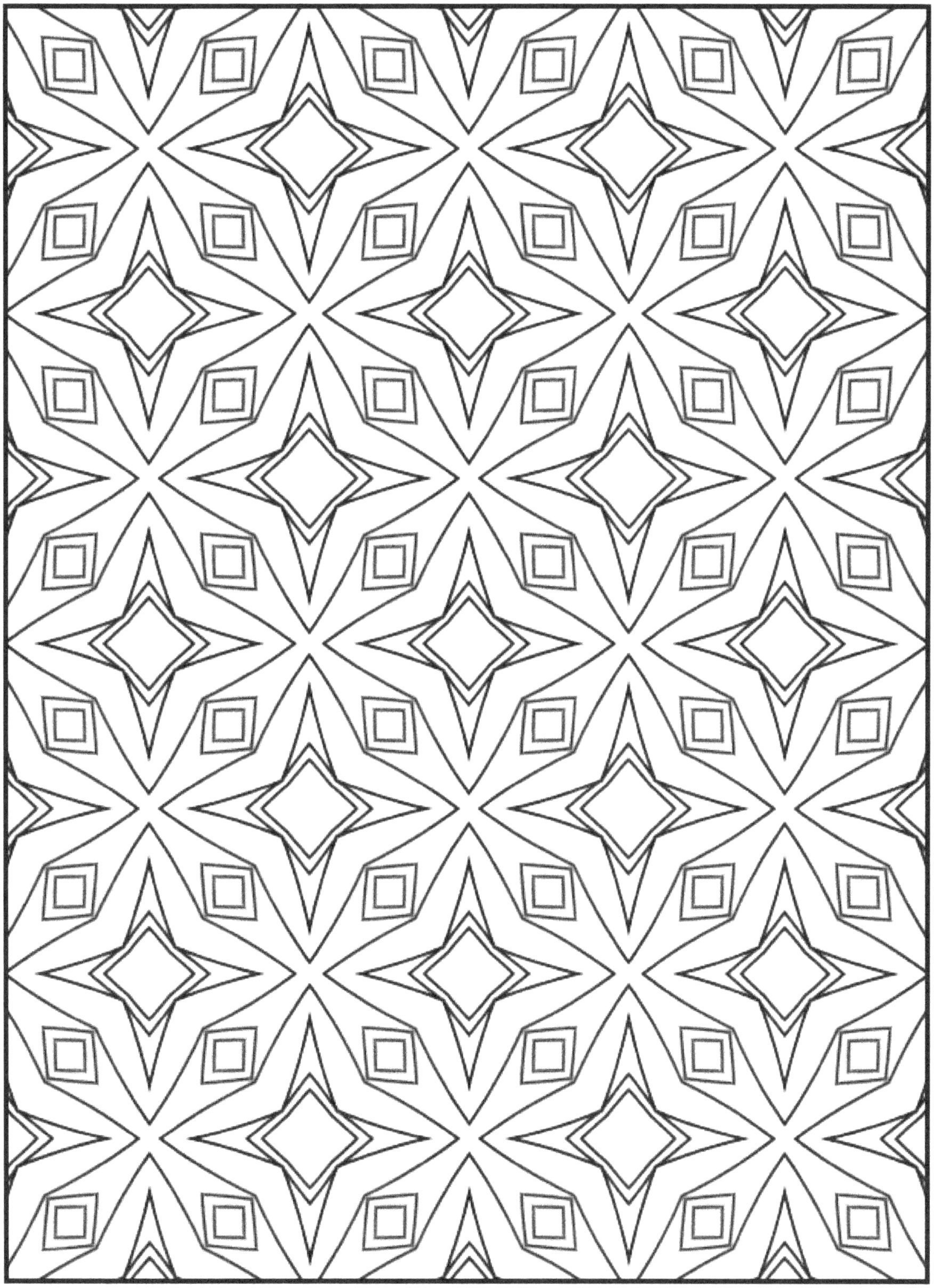

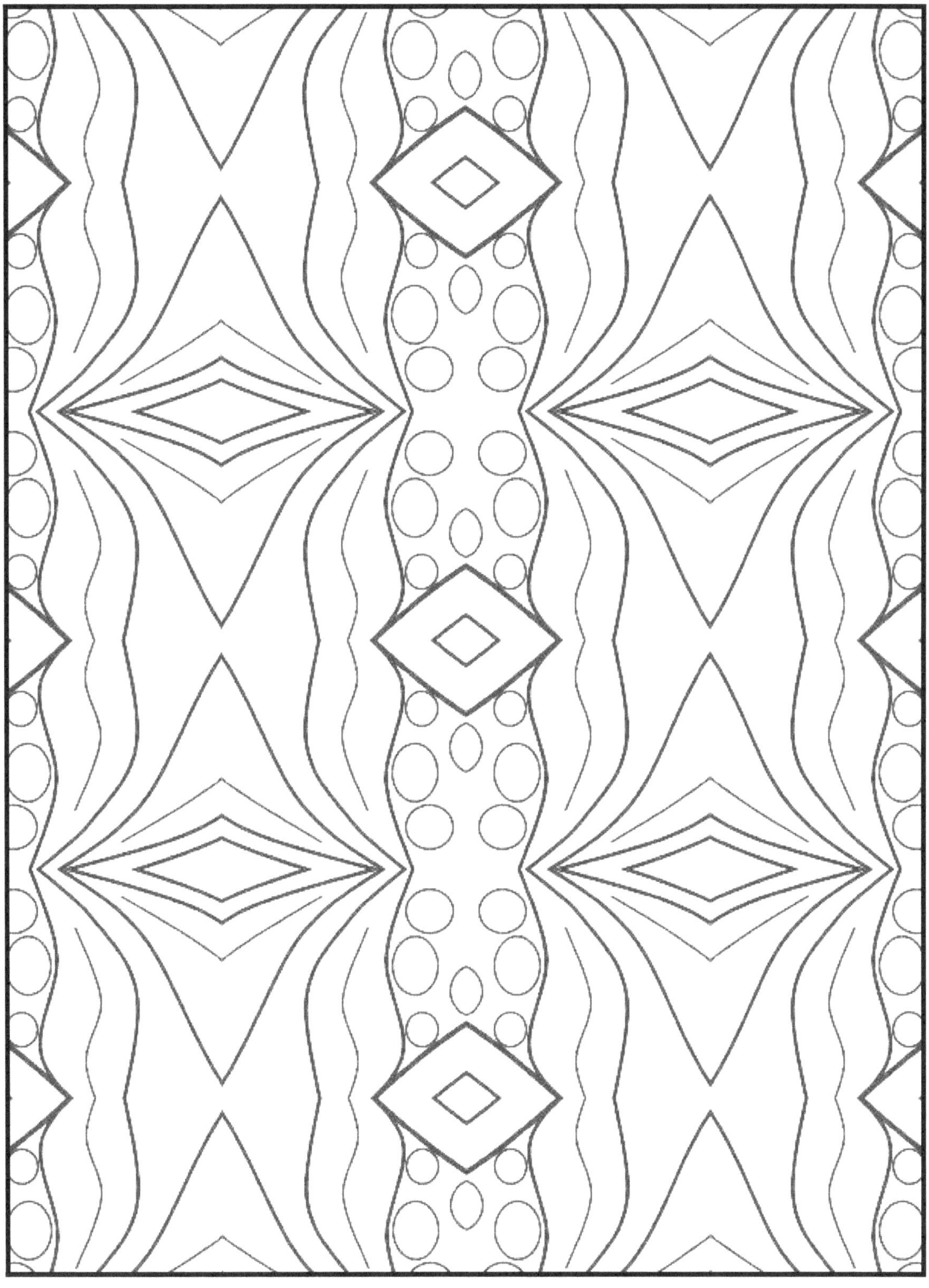

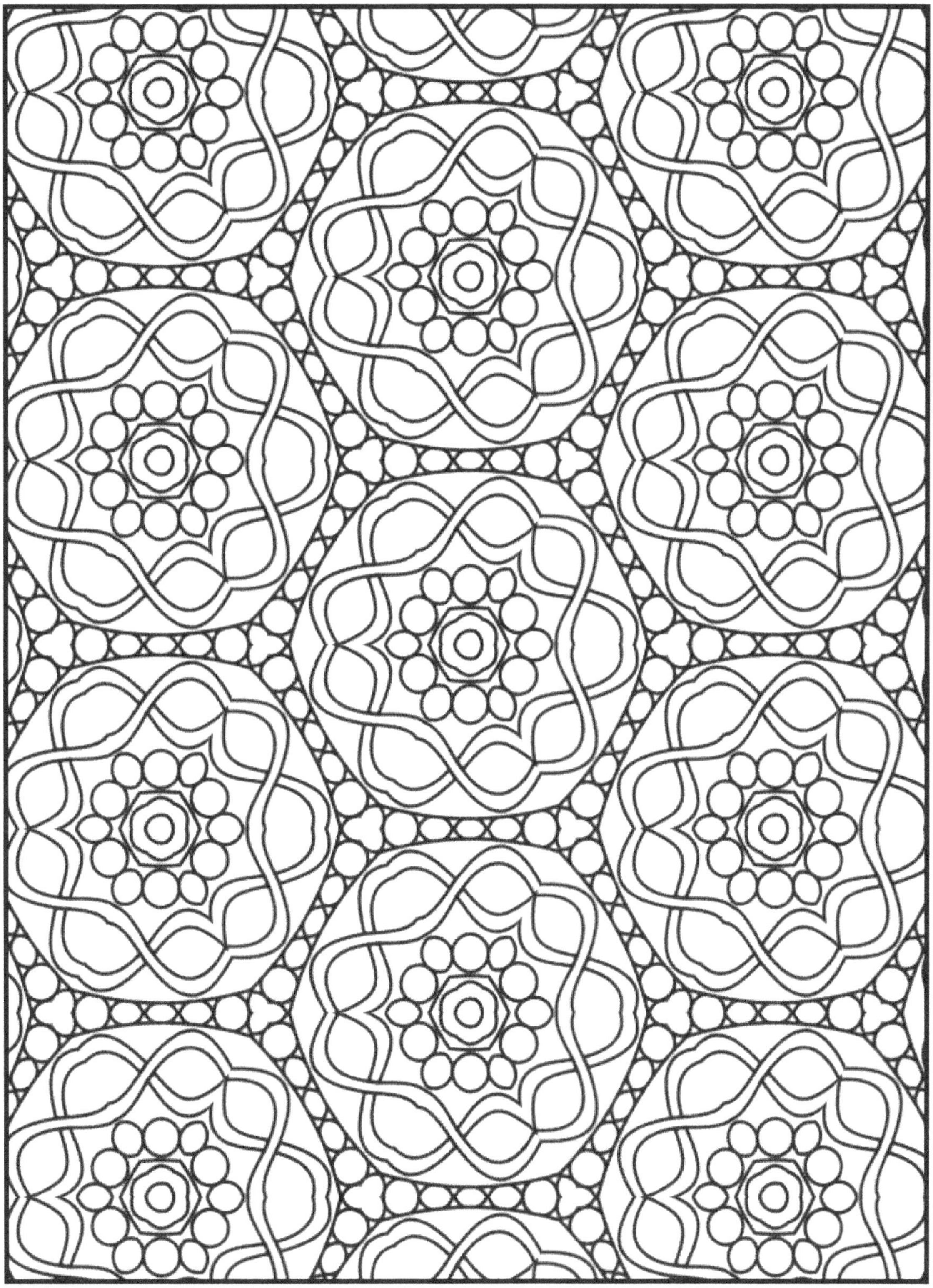

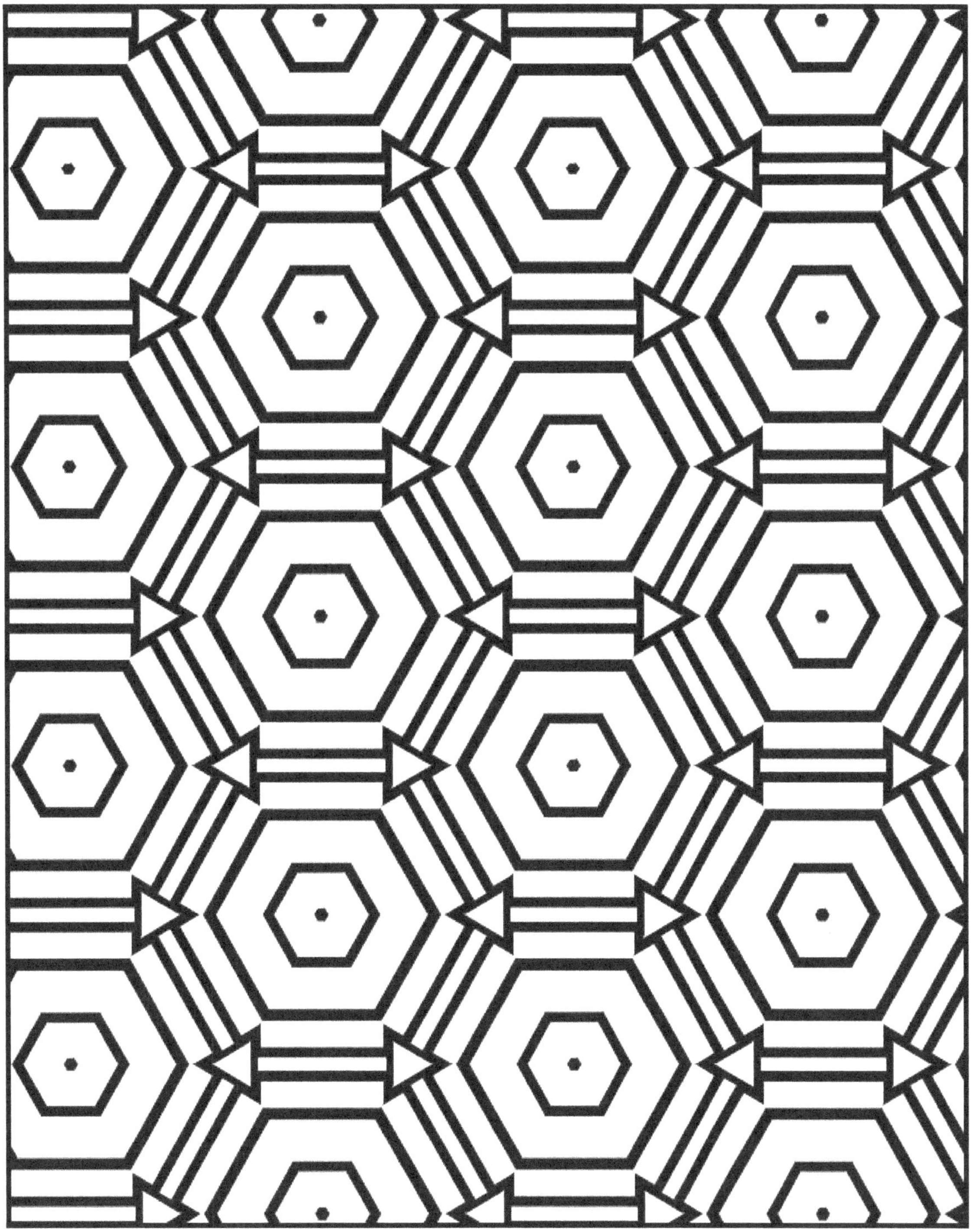

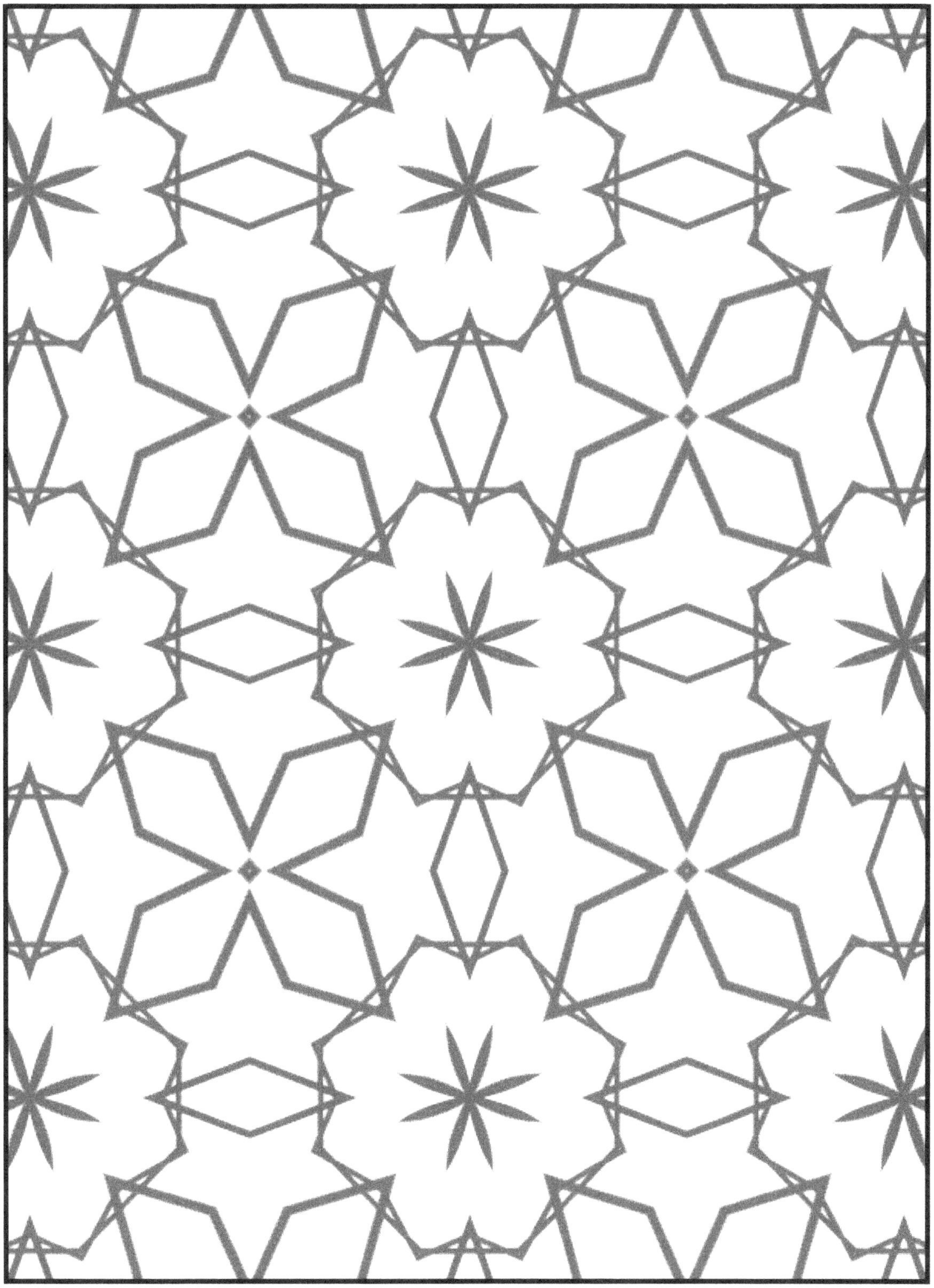

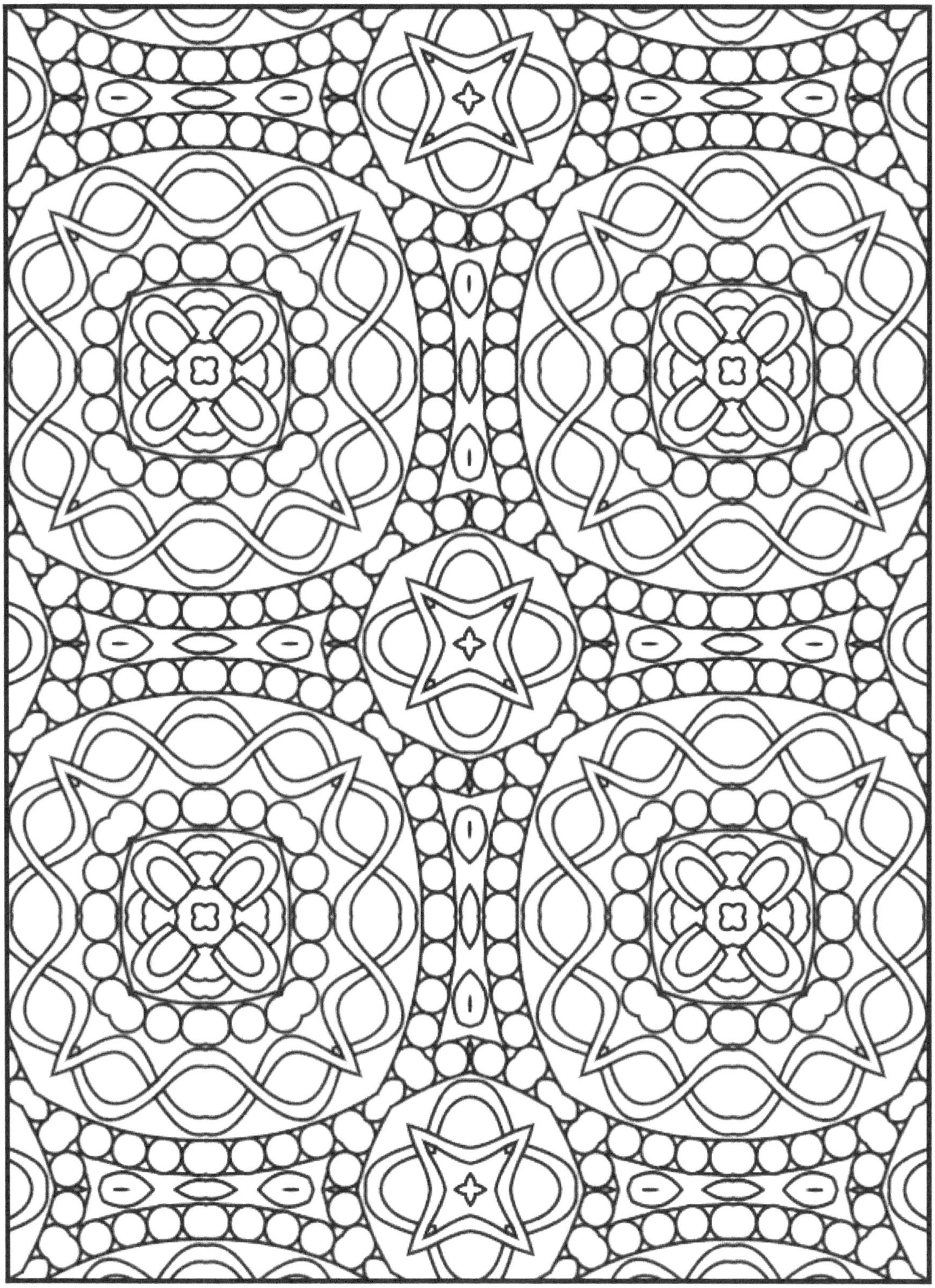

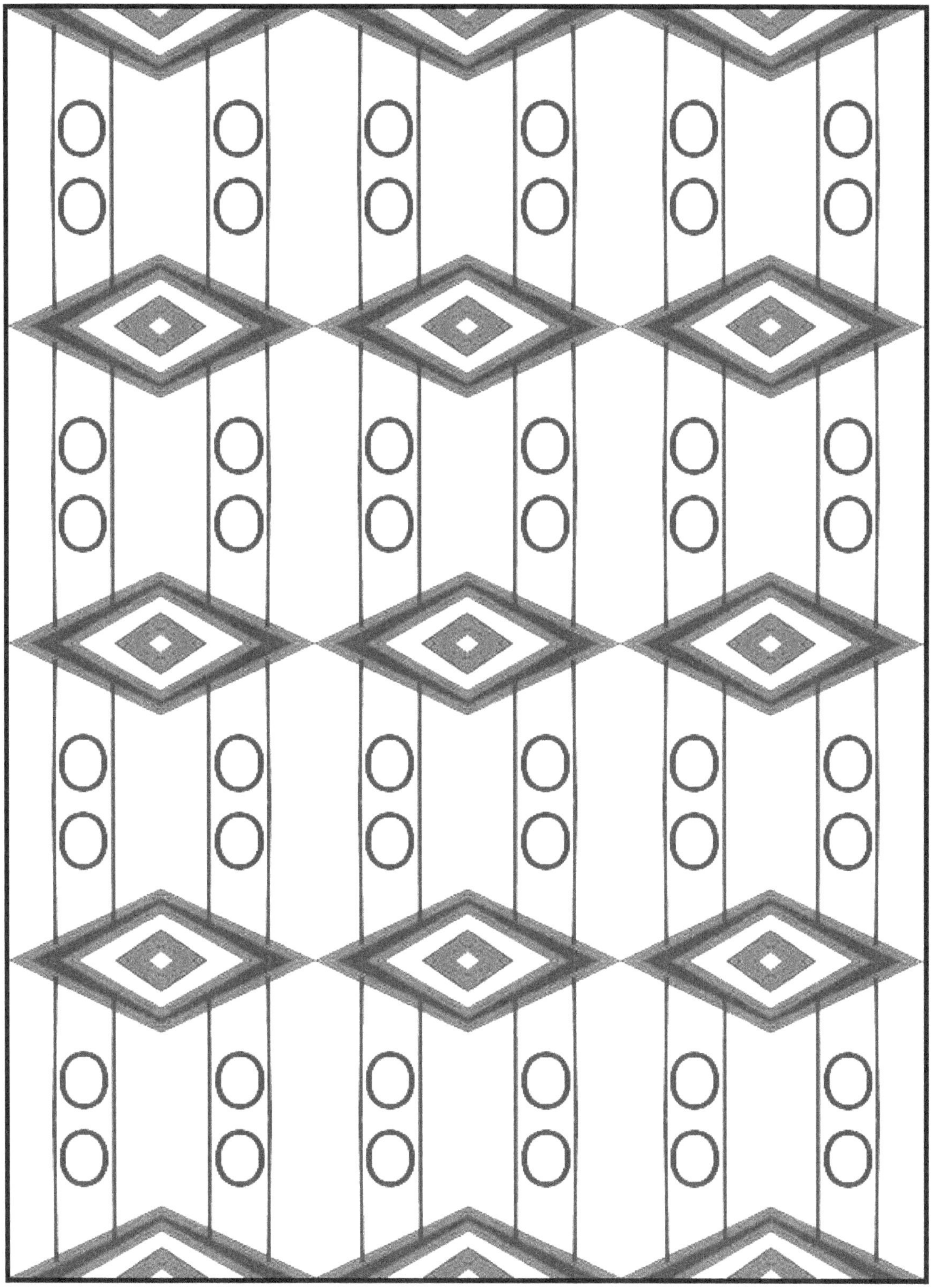

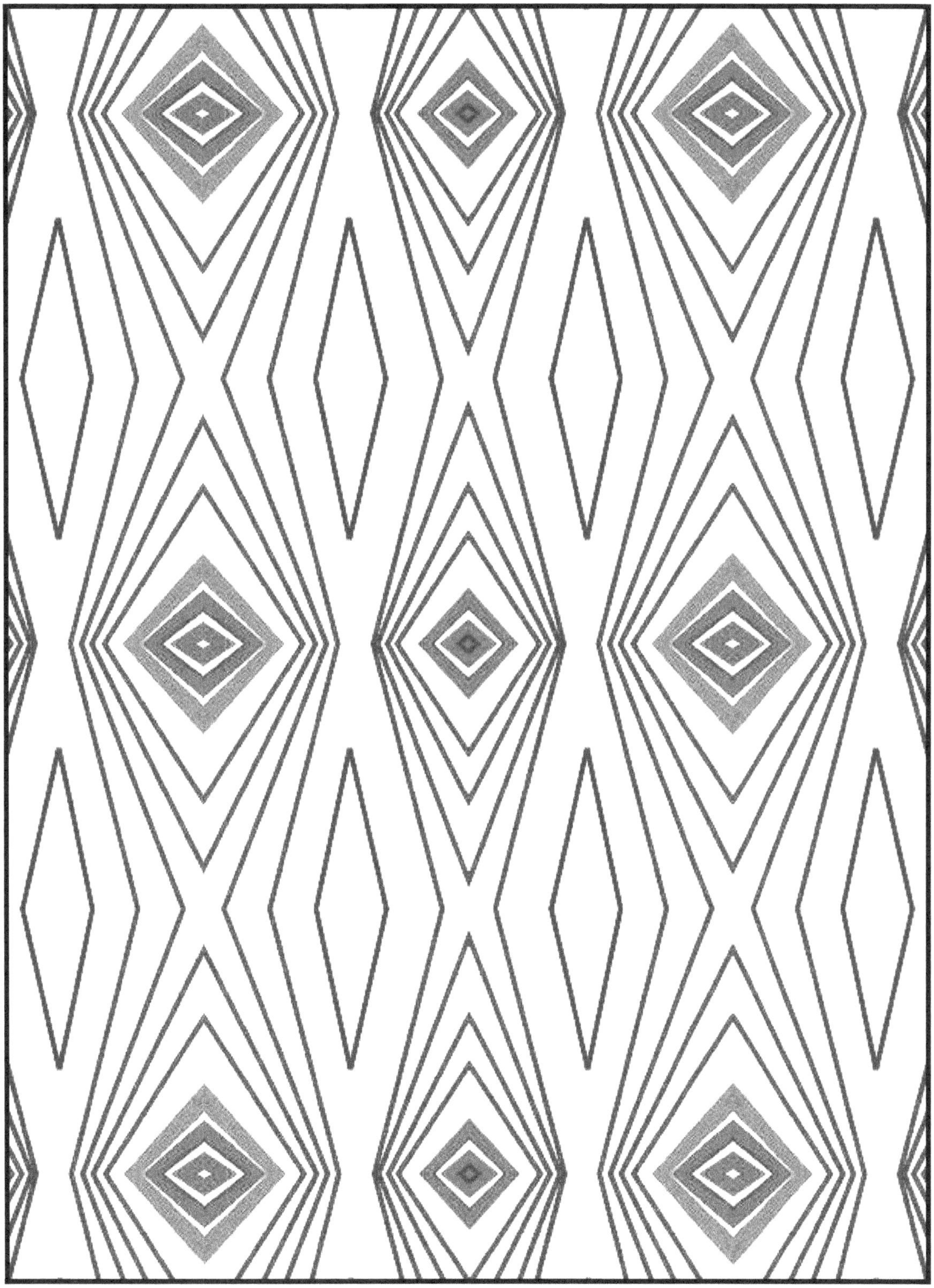

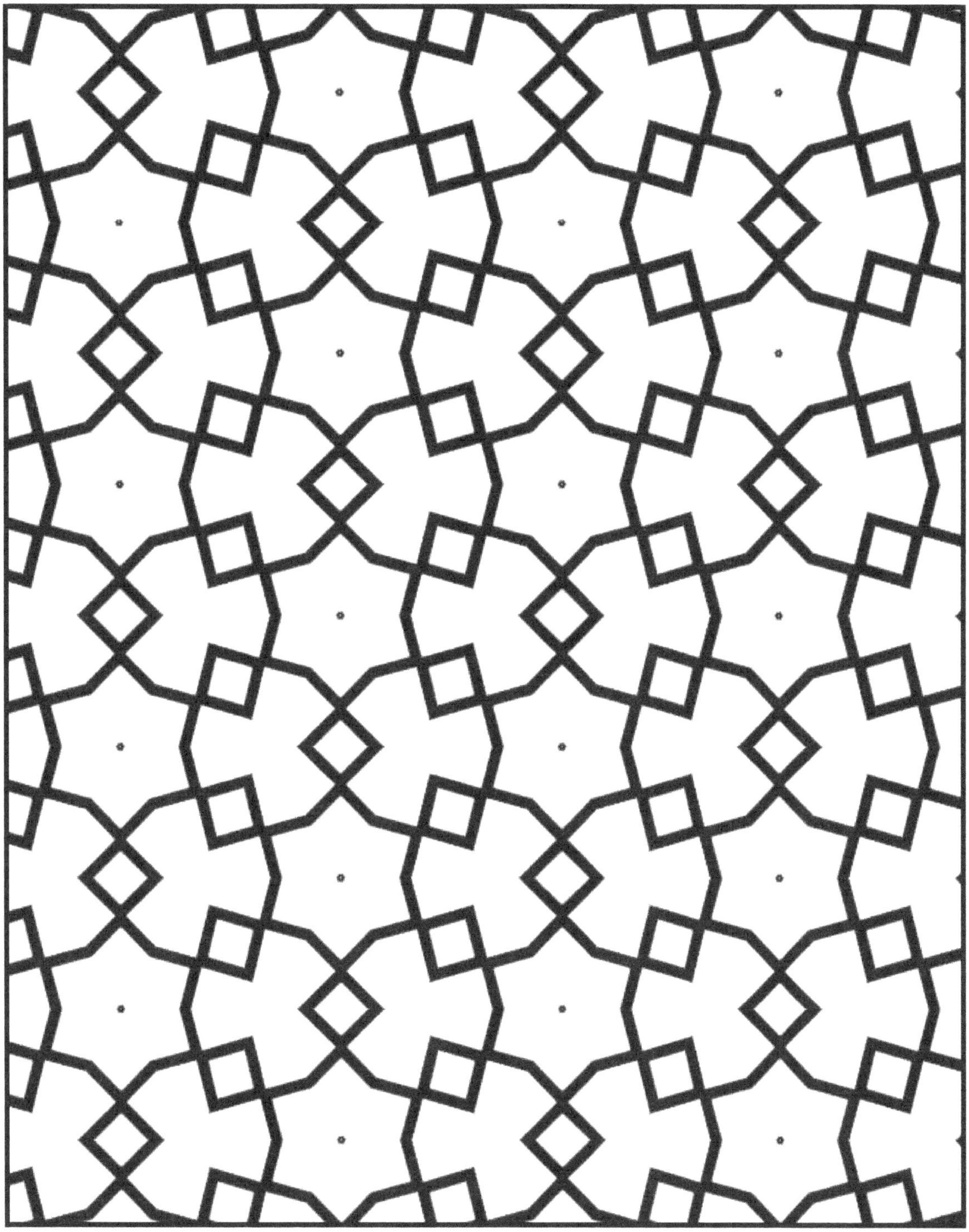

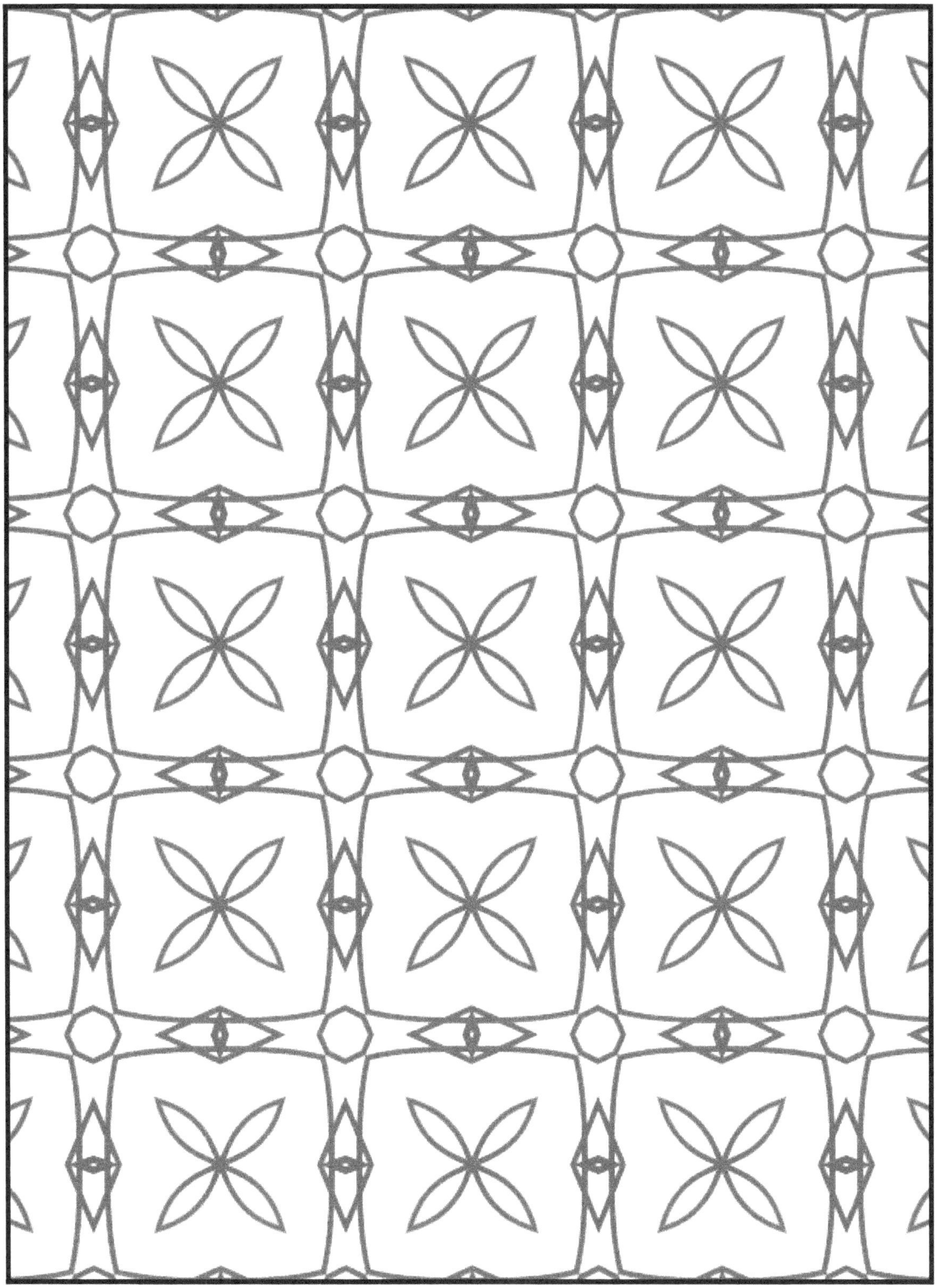

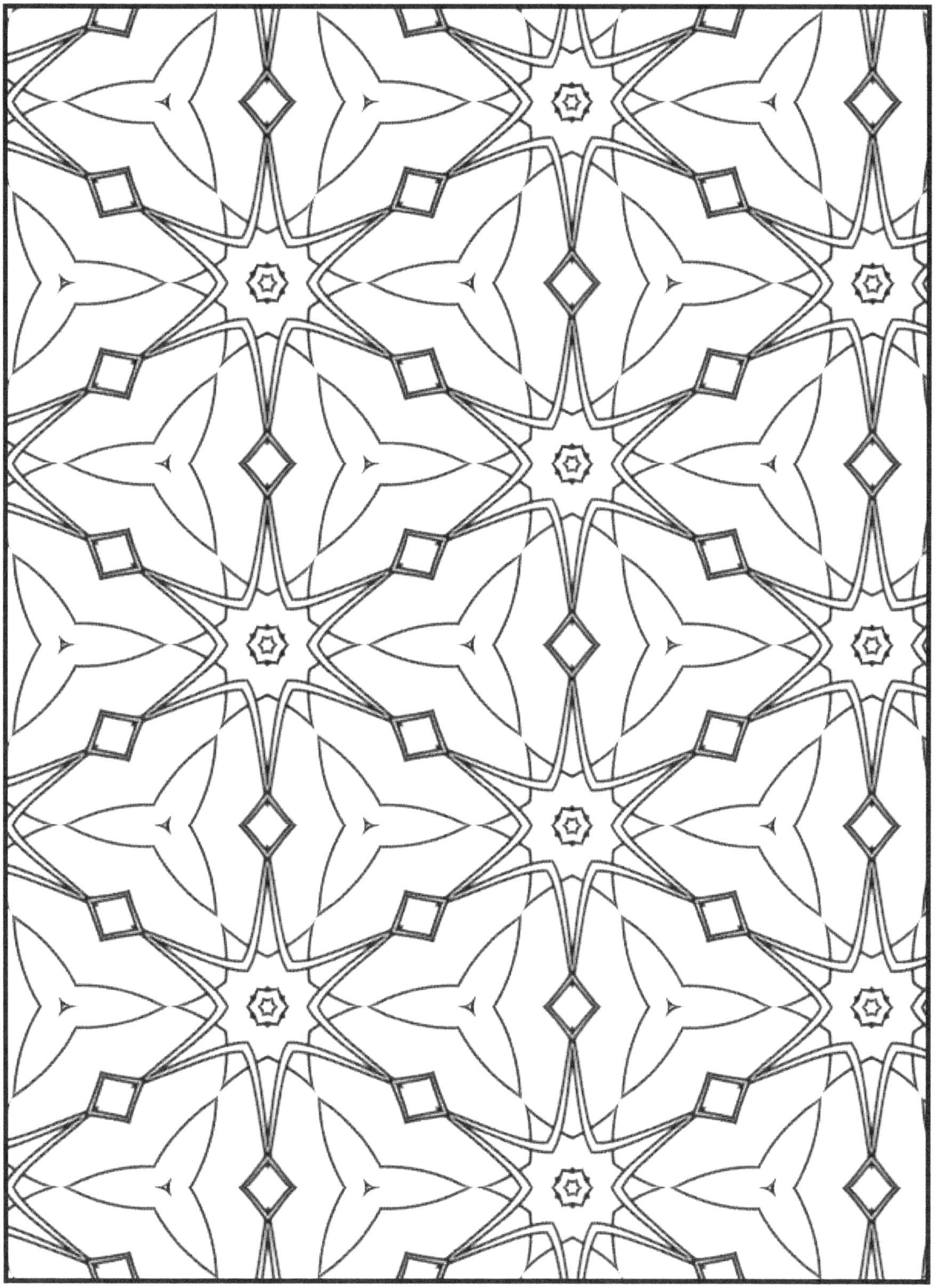

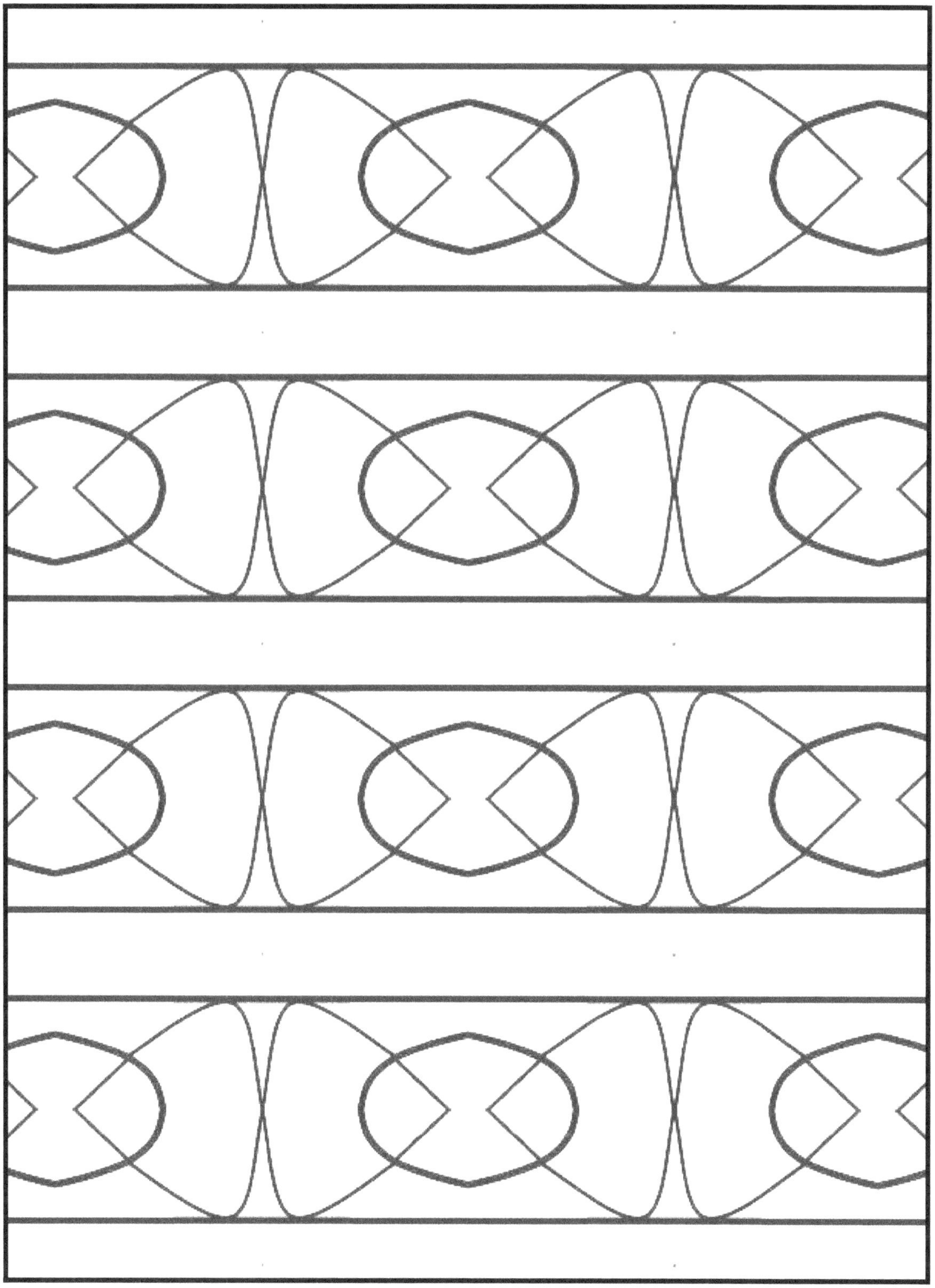

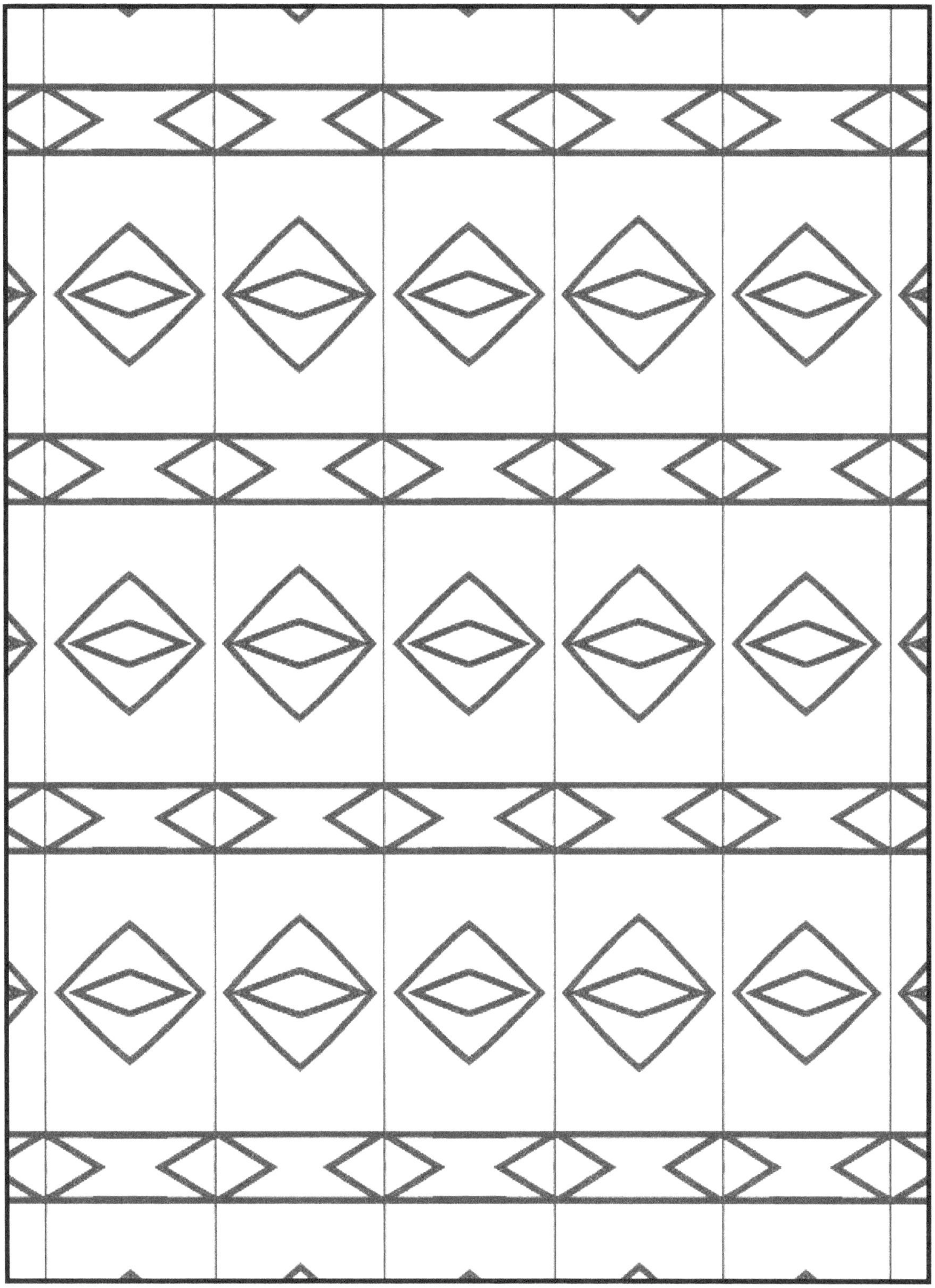

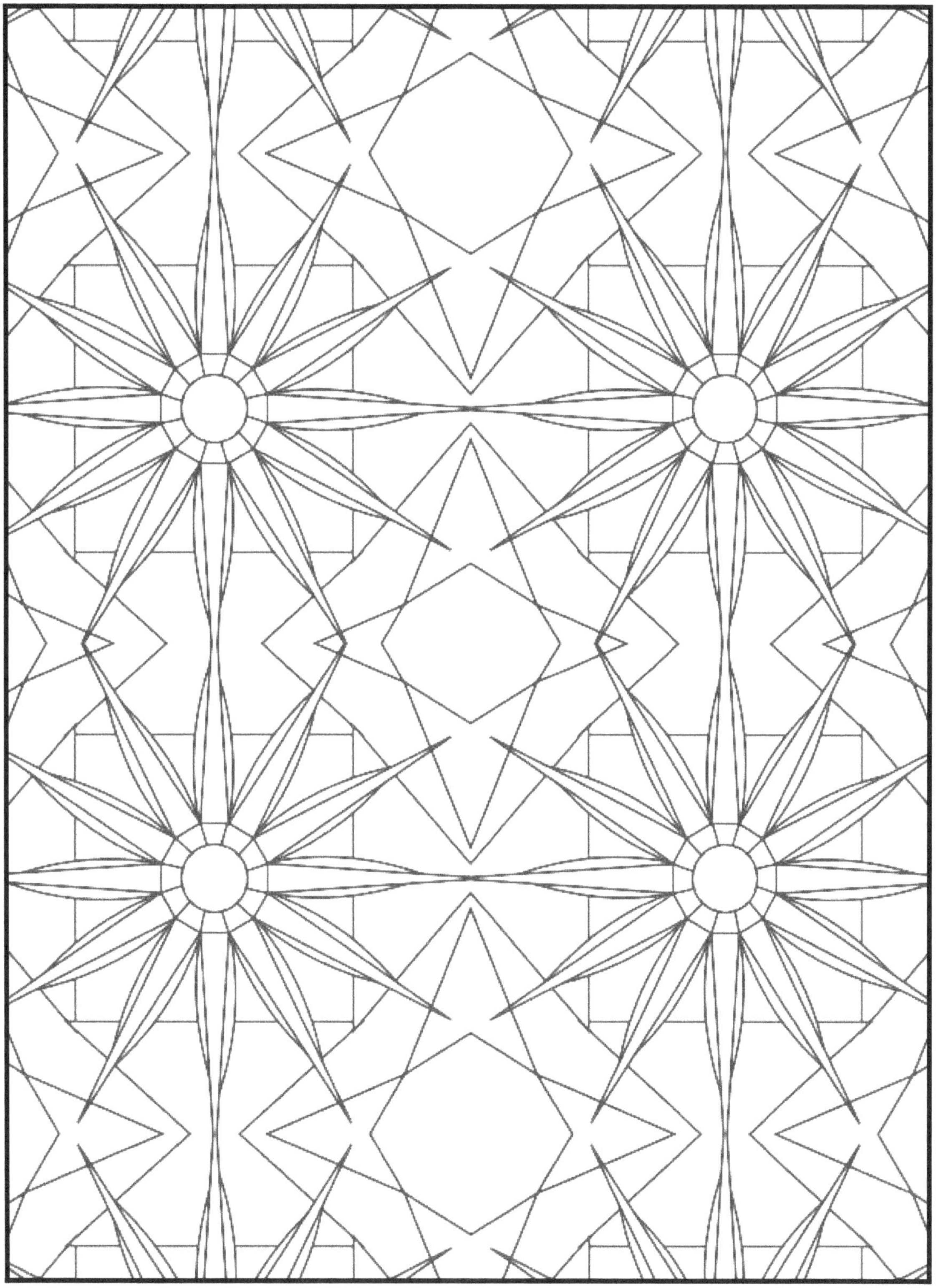

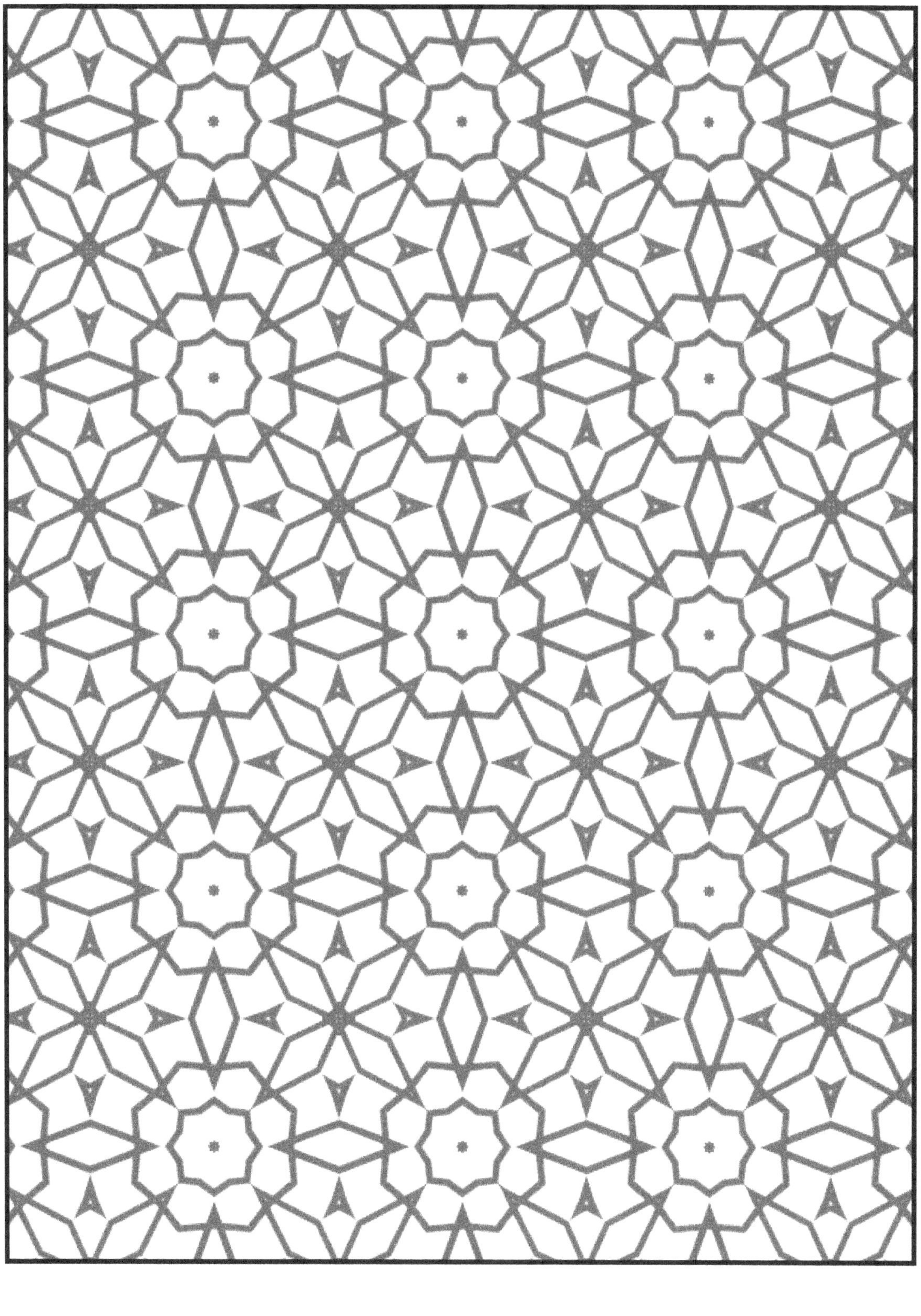

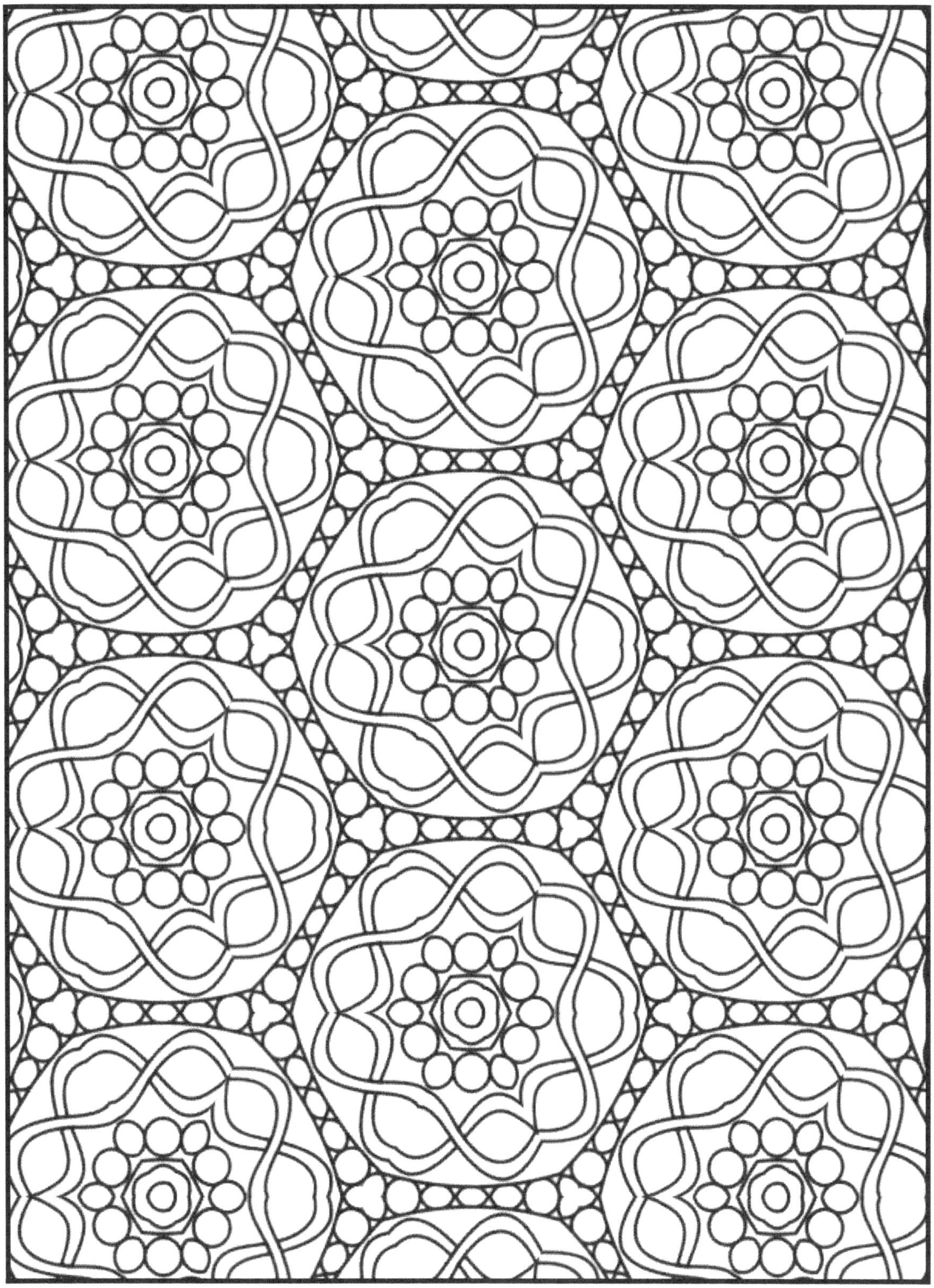

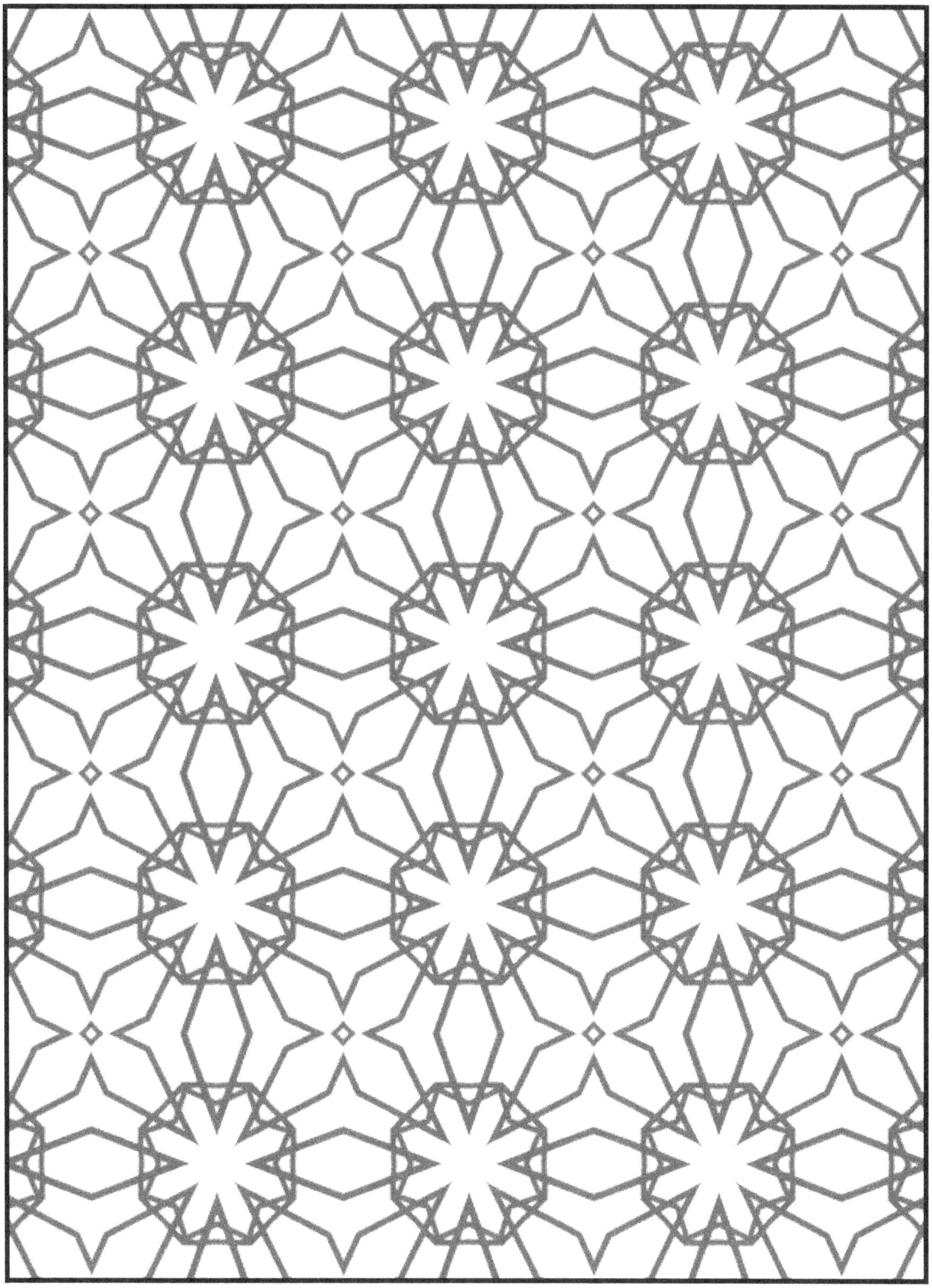

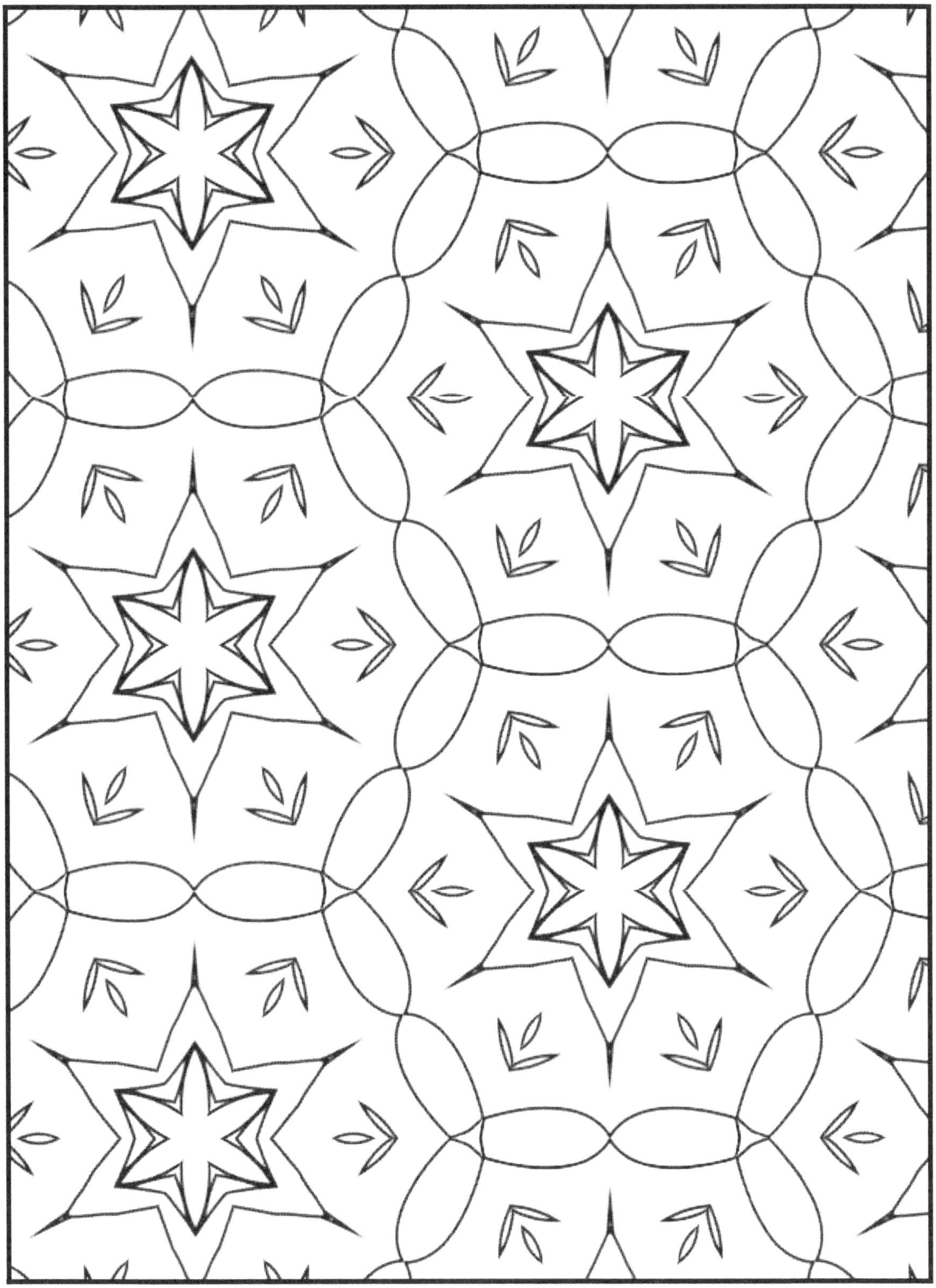

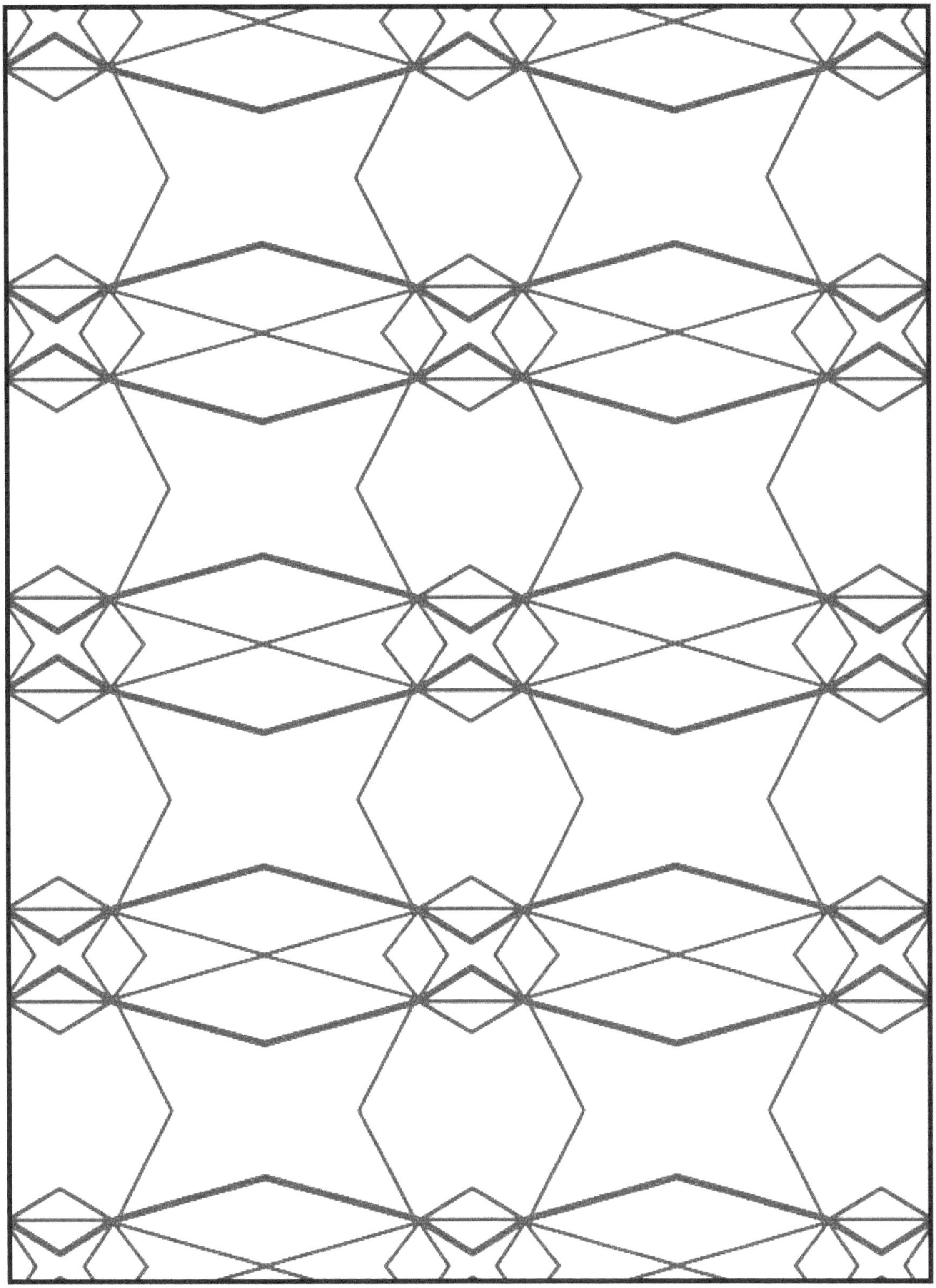

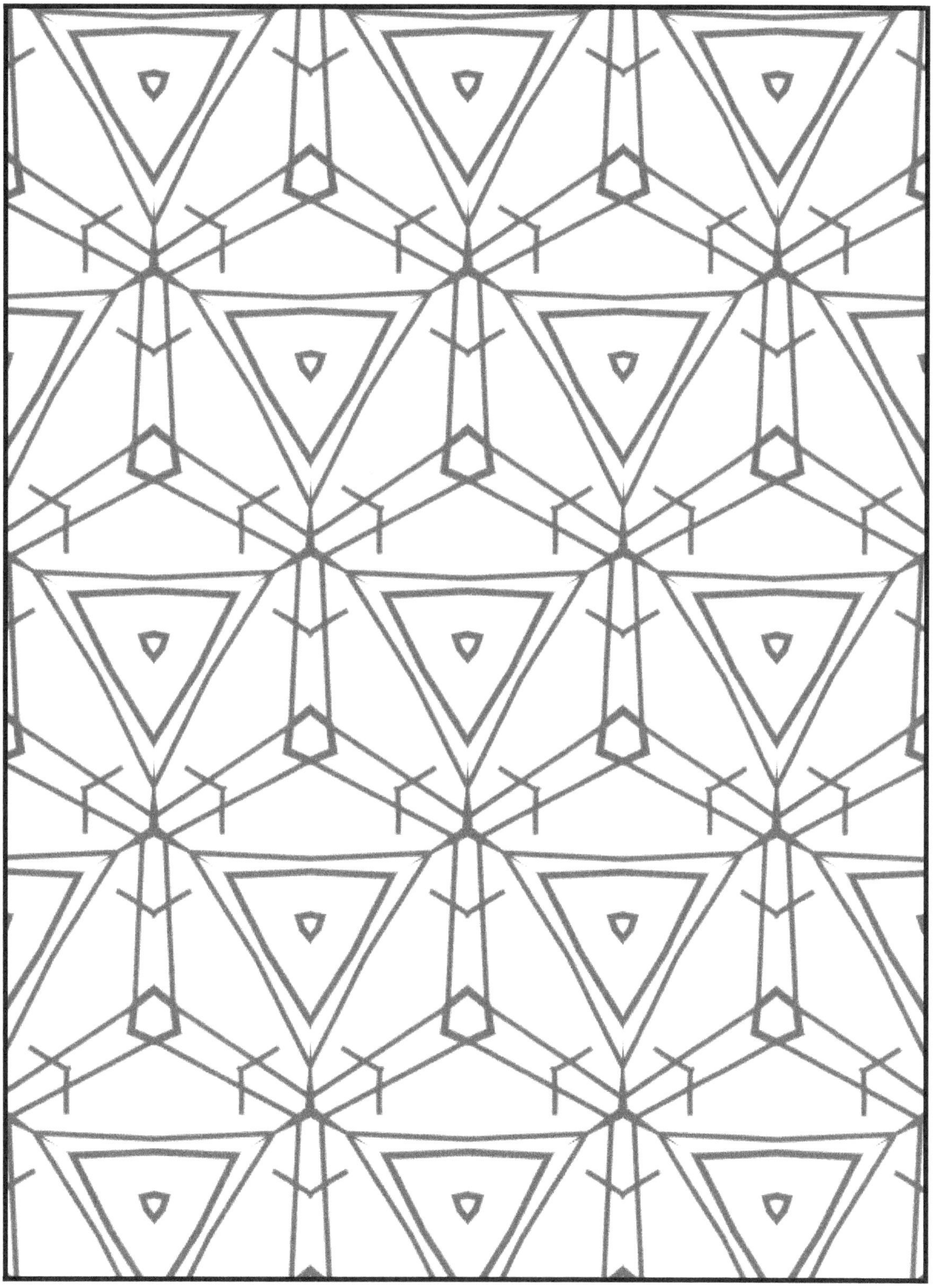

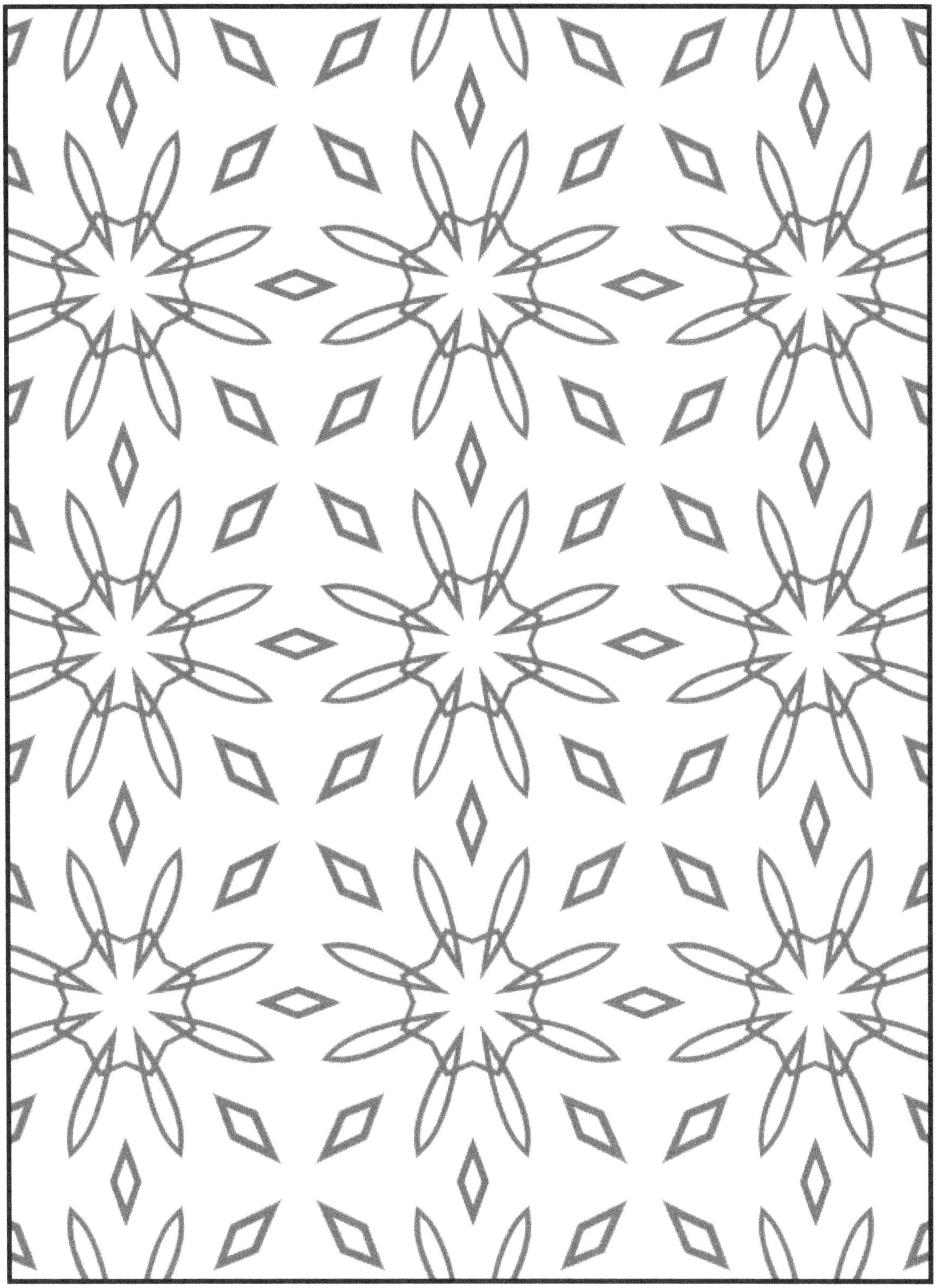

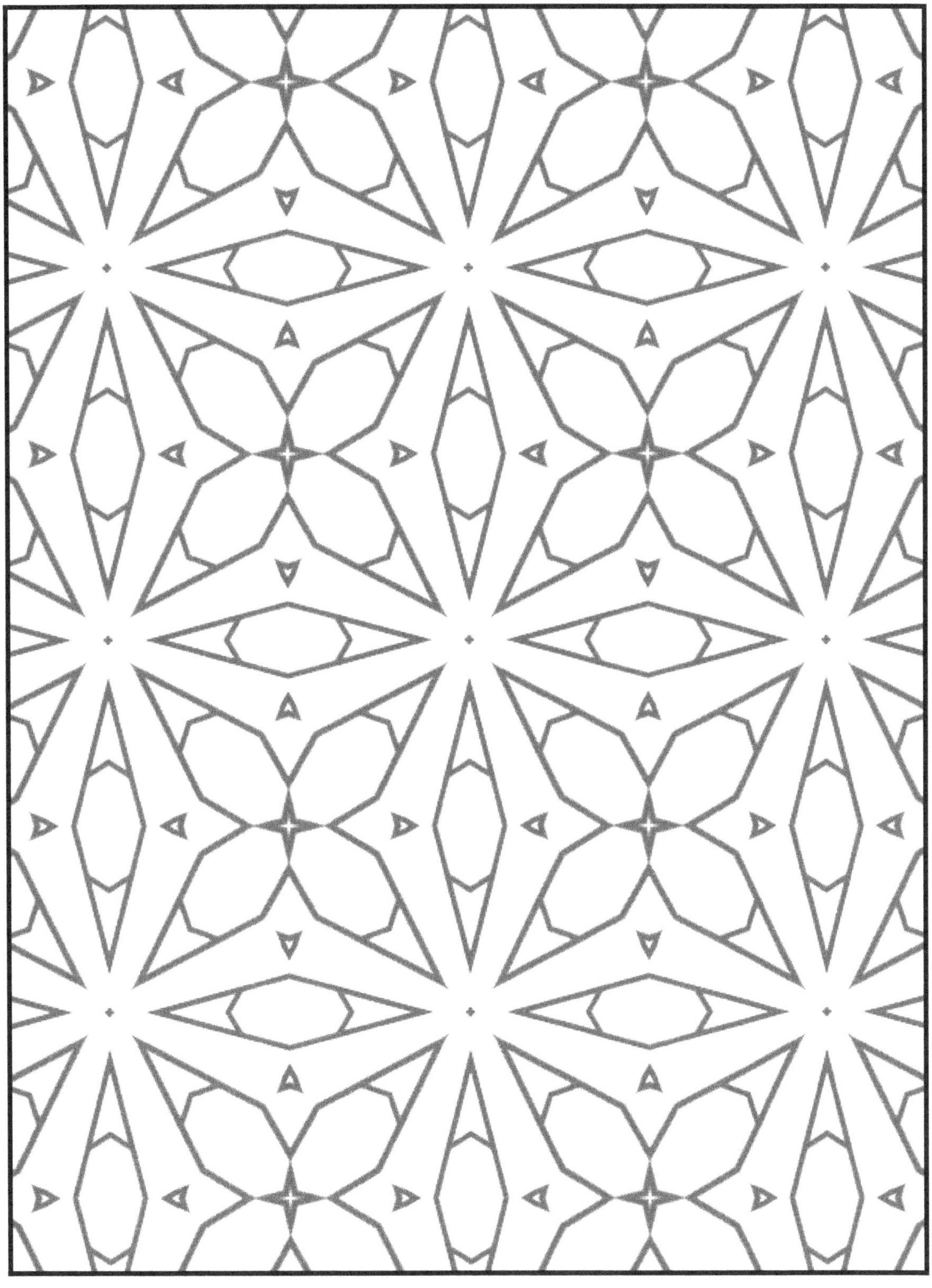

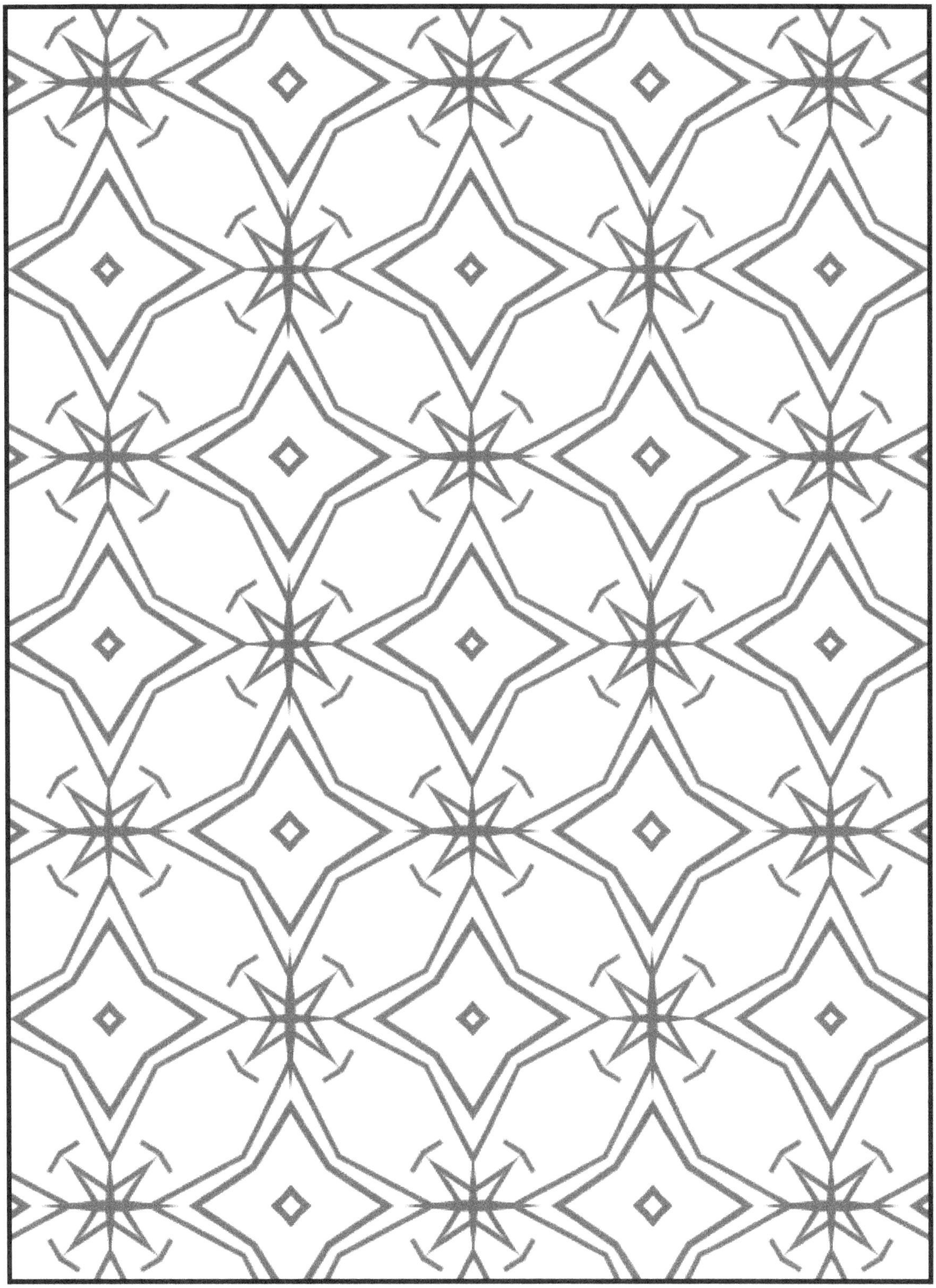

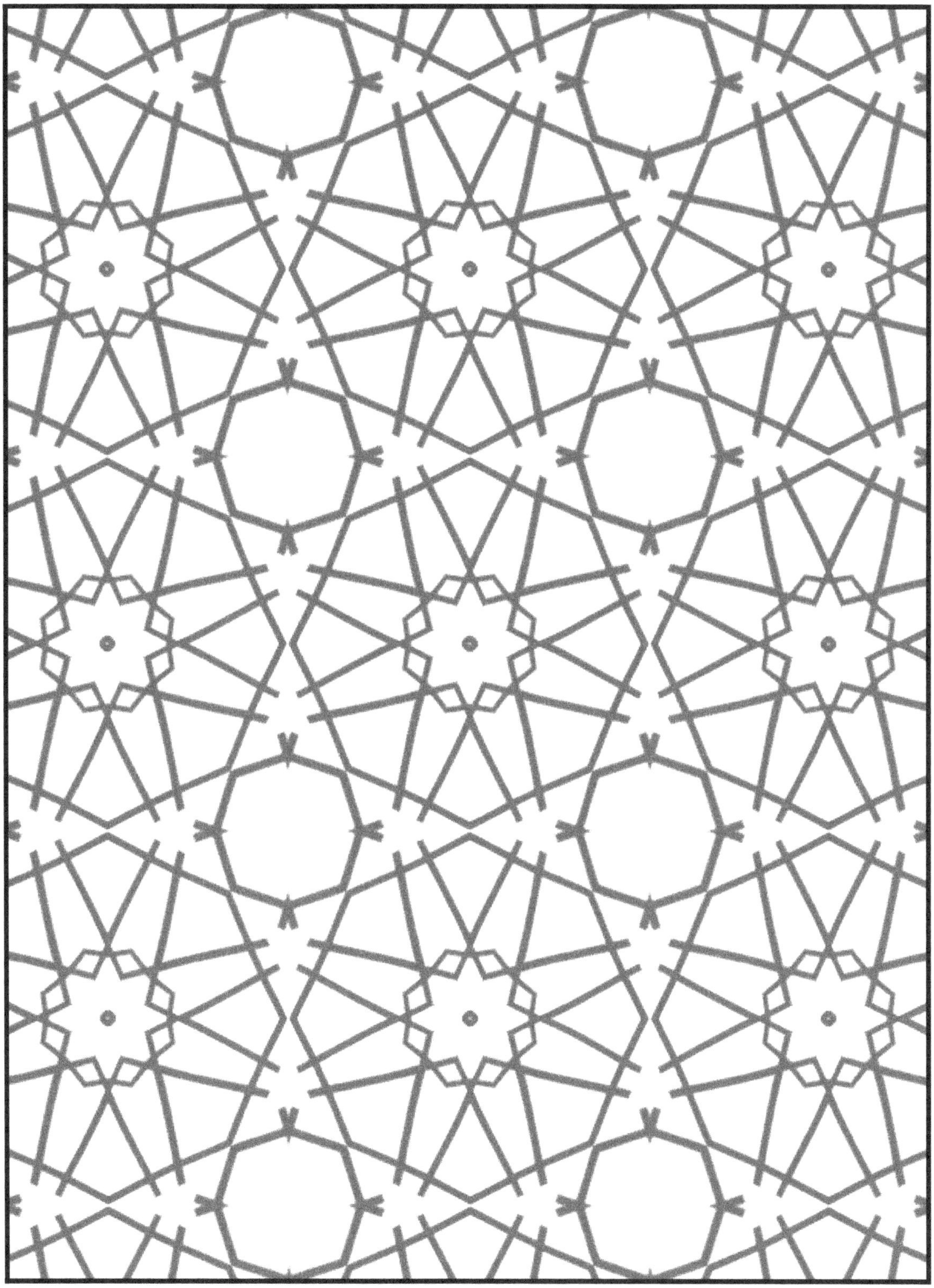

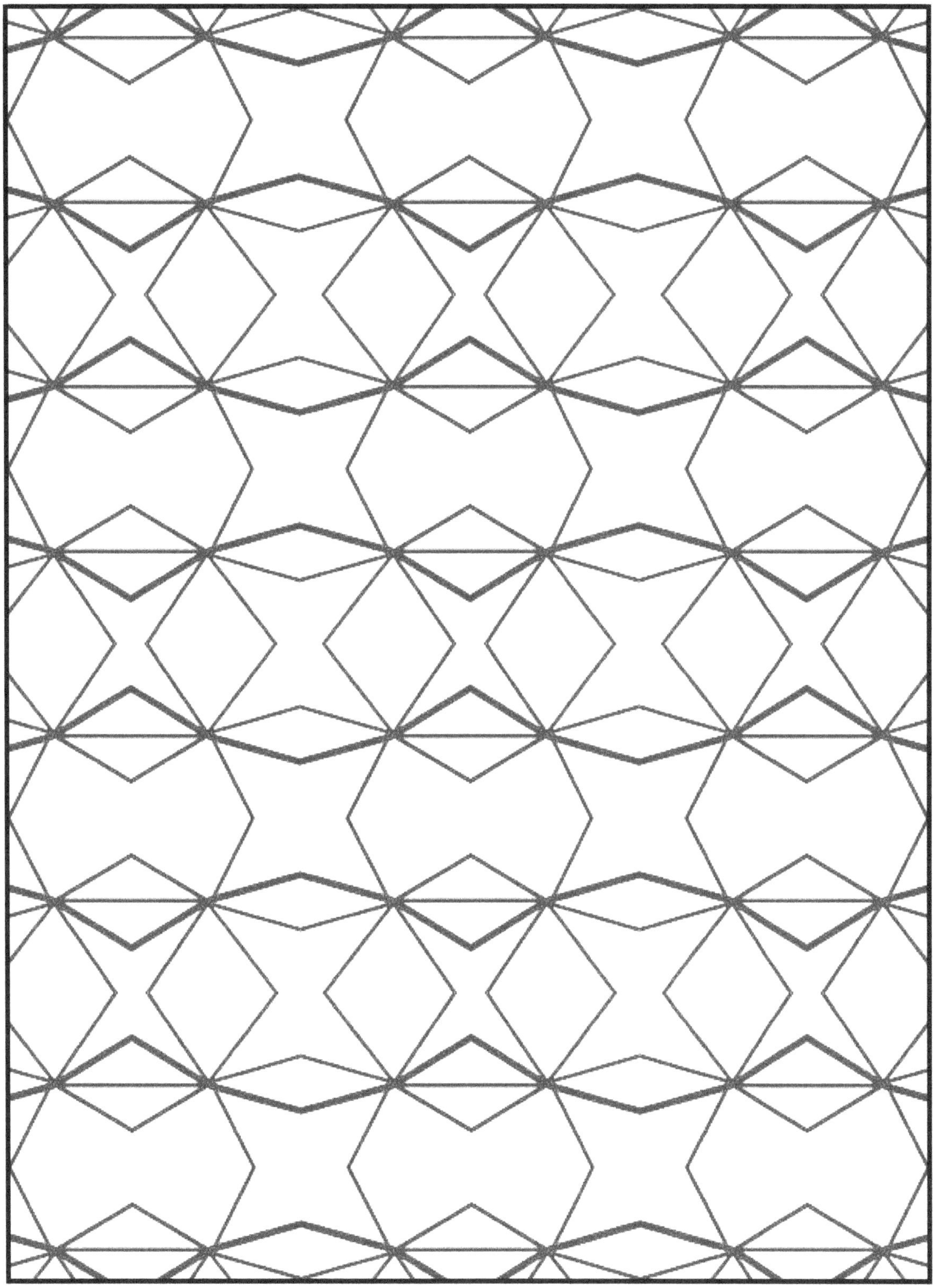

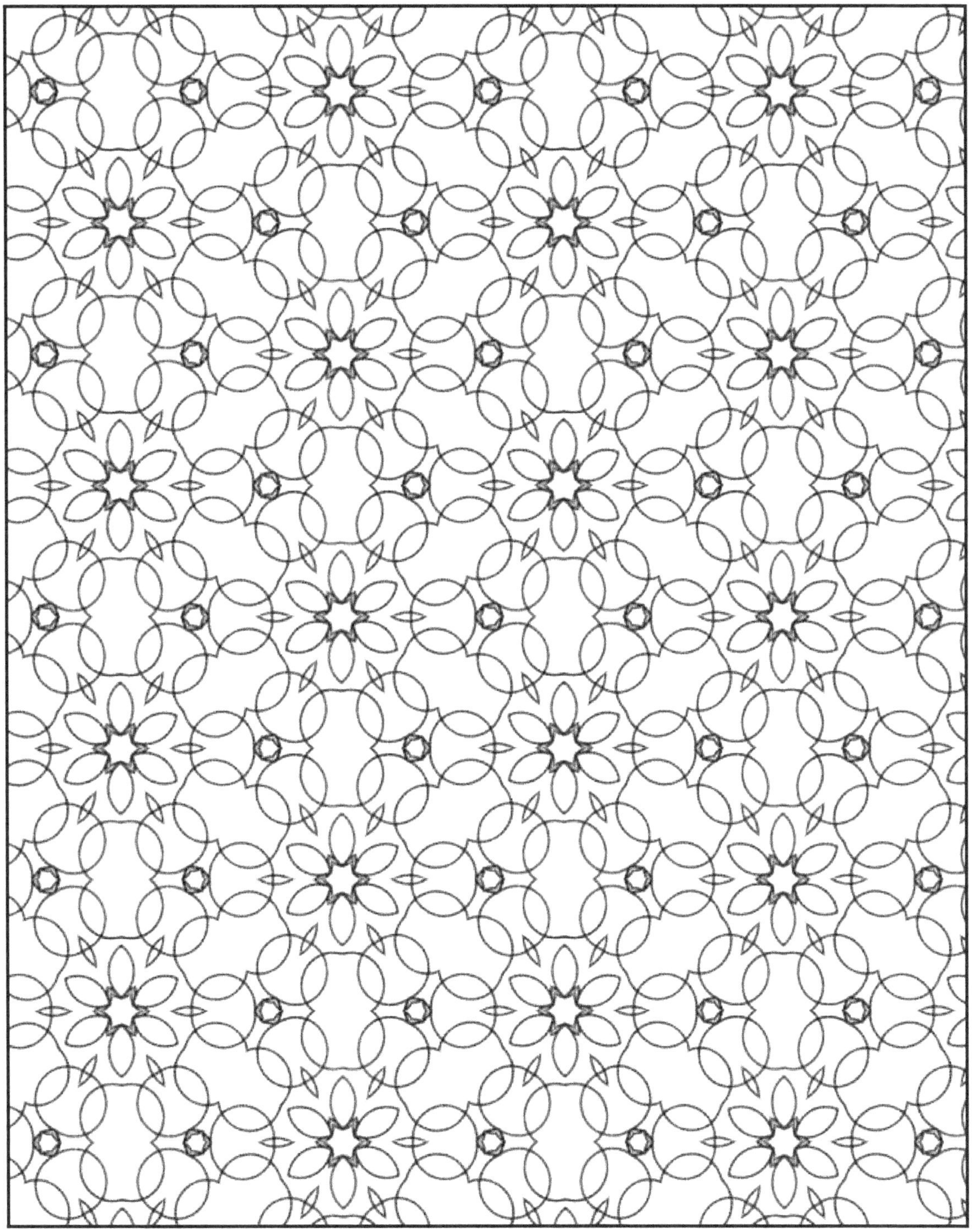

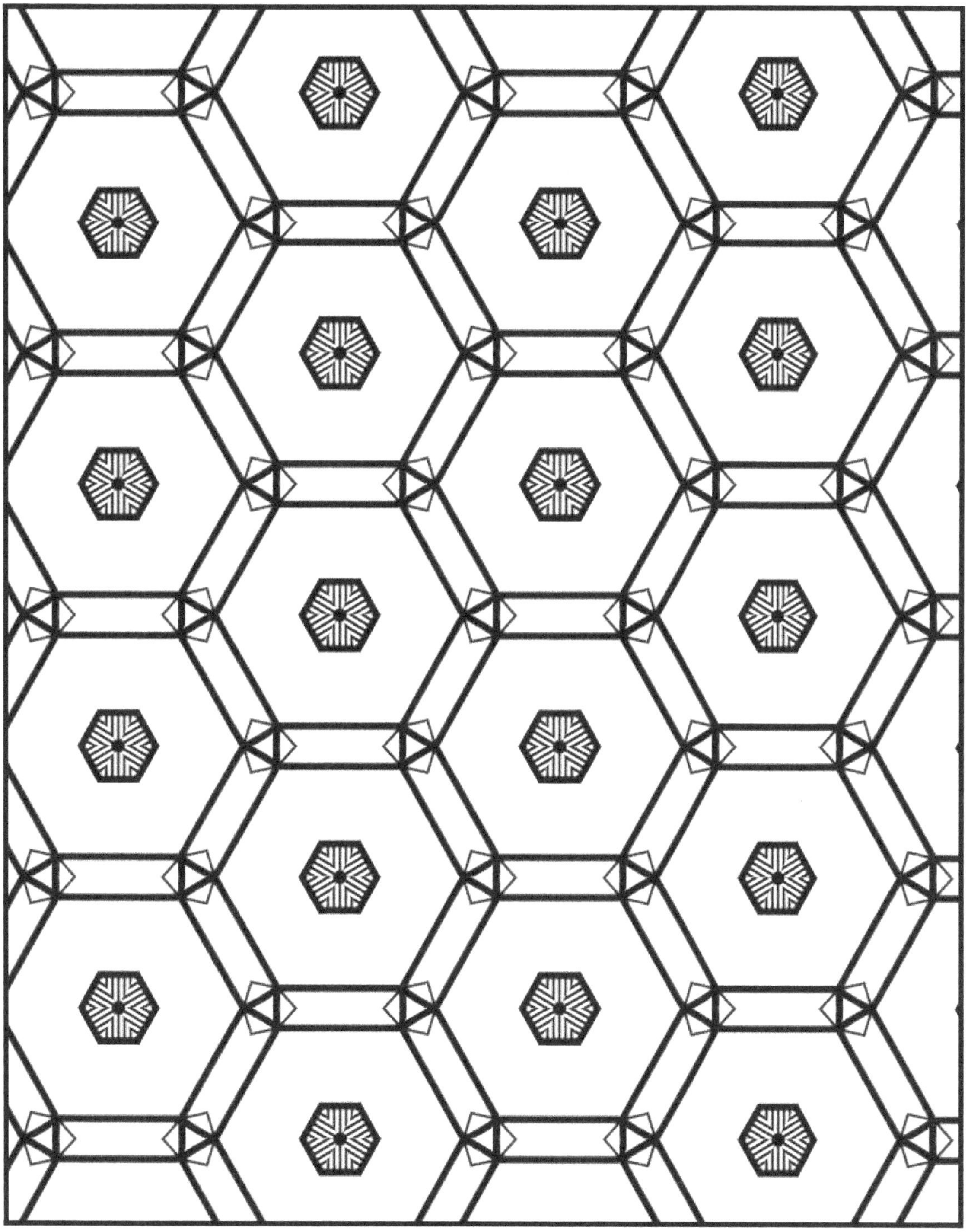

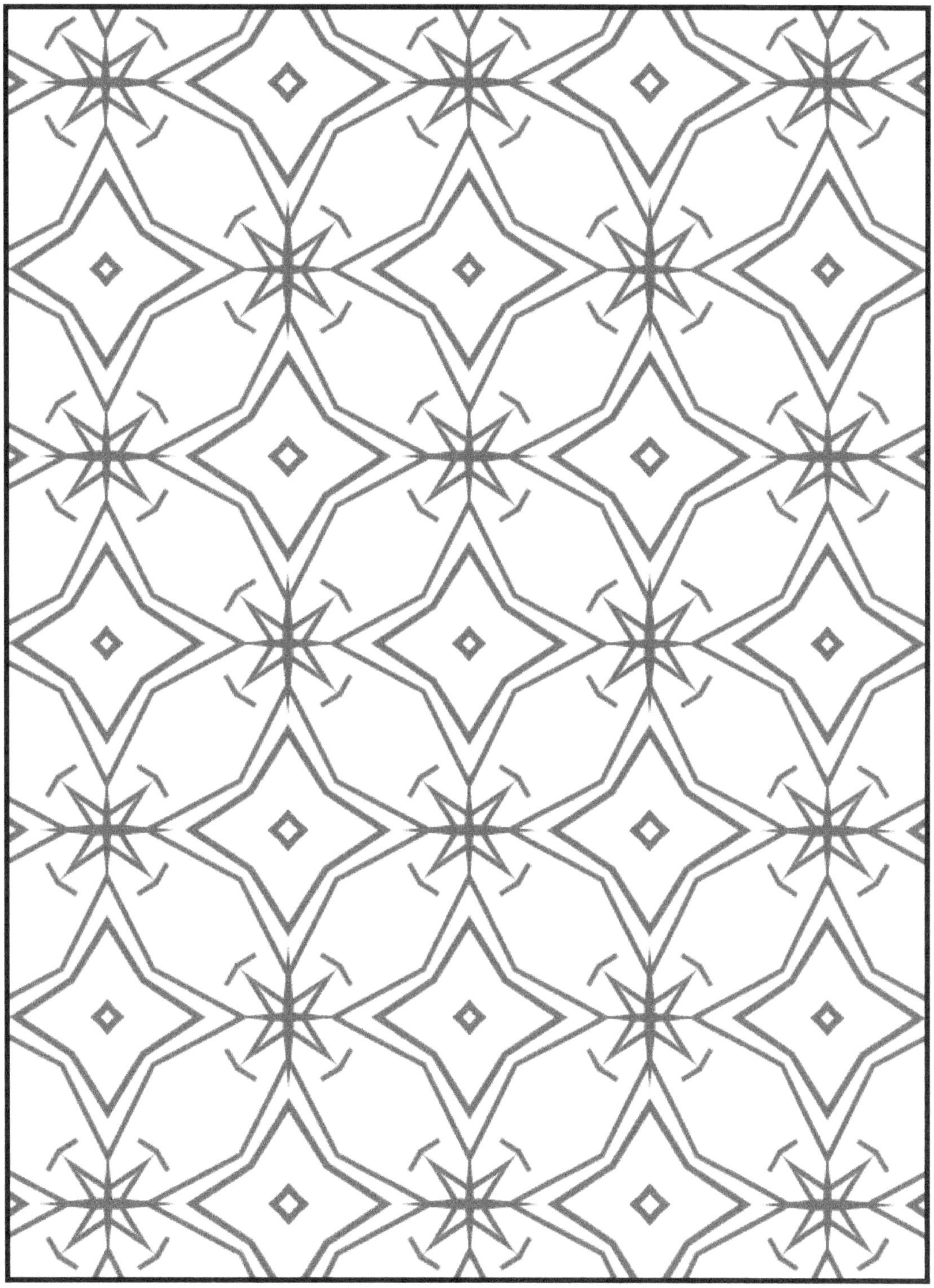

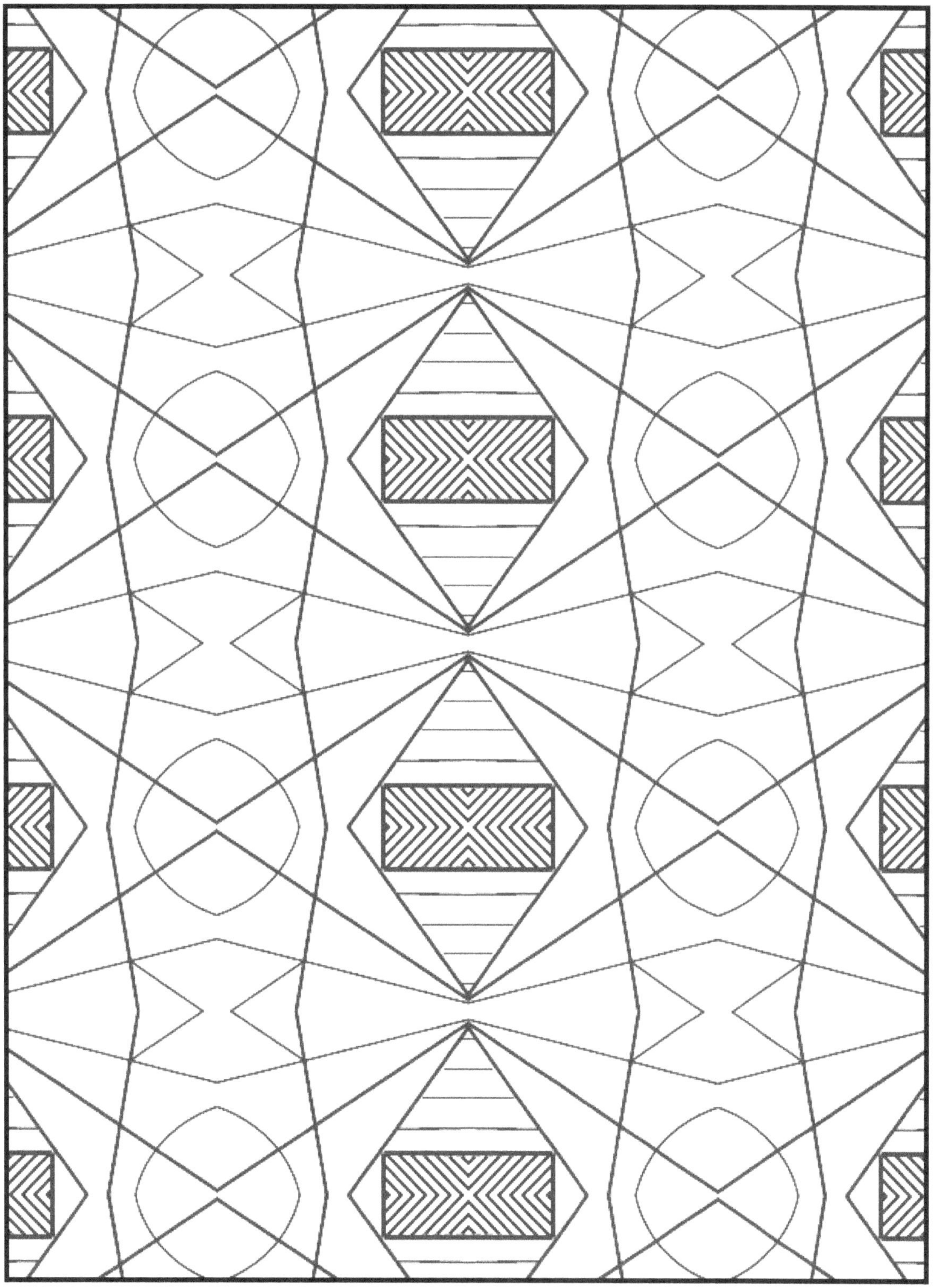

For More Books From Our Publishing Company Including Other Authors and Illustrators Visit http://kdcoloring.com

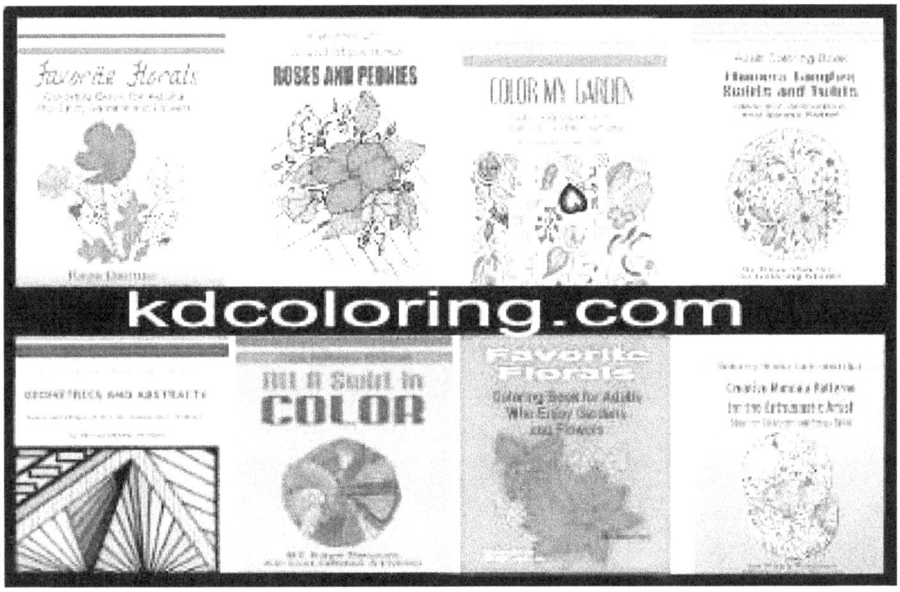

www.ingramcontent.com/pod-product-compliance
Lightning Source LLC
Chambersburg PA
CBHW081607200526
45169CB00021B/2213